The Mystery FANcier

WILLIAM POWELL as PHILO VANCE

Volume 2, Number 2
March 1978

The MYSTERY FANcIER

Volume 2 Number 2
March 1978

TABLE OF CONTENTS

MYSTERIOUSLY SPEAKING 1
The Matt Helm Series, by Banks and Townsend 3
Professor Without a Pseudonym, by Larry L. French . . 12
Bouchercon VIII: Murder at the Waldorf, by Mary
    Ann Grochowski 15
Miscellaneous Mystery Mish-Mash, Part II: The
    California Switch, by Marvin Lachman 19
The (Very Temporary) Return of Skull-Face, by
    Robert E. Briney 21
The Nero Wolfe Saga, Part VI, by Guy M. Townsend. . . 25
MYSTERY*FILE: Short Reviews by Steve Lewis. 33
VERDICTS (More Reviews) 36
THE DOCUMENTS IN THE CASE (Letters) 41

The MYSTERY FANcier
is edited and published by Guy M. Townsend,
1596 Hester Road, Memphis, TN 38116, USA.
Contributions of all descriptions welcomed.
Deadline for May issue: 1 April 1978.

Subscription rates: Domestic first class mail, $7.50 per year (6 issues); Overseas surface mail, $7.50; Overseas air mail, $12,000. Overseas subscribers please pay in international money order, check drawn on U.S. bank, or currency; no checks drawn on foreign banks, please. Make checks payable to Guy M. Townsend—I get some strange looks when I try to cash checks made out to "The Mystery Fancier".

ADVERTISING RATES: full page $10.00; half page $7.00; quarter page $4.00; eighth page and smaller $2.00. Small ads will be retyped; quarter page and larger ads will be e-stenciled as submitted, so illustrations—provided they contain no large black areas—may be included.

Cover by Franklyn Hamilton

Copyright 1978 by Guy M. Townsend
All rights reserved for contributors
ISSN:0146-3160

MYSTERIOUSLY SPEAKING . . .

    The readability of TMF 2:1 was so bad that I was embarrassed to mail it out. I did, though, because I couldn't afford the time or the money it would have taken to redo it. A number of factors were responsible for the rotten reproduction of that issue. First, my IBM Selectric I, an ancient machine, was designed to use fabric ribbons rather than carbon ones (carbon ribbons *were* available for it, but only at a prohibitively high cost), and I always purchased a new ribbon before typing up each issue. Unfortunately, the "new" ribbon that I purchased before typing 2:1 was very, very faint. I noticed this when I began to type the issue, but it was during a weekend when it would have been difficult, though not impossible, to buy another one, and I typed so much over that weekend that it would have been too much work for me to retype it again. I kidded myself that my electro-stencil cutter would make it come out all right. I was mistaken, particularly so since my e-stencil machine needed a new stylus and I didn't notice it until I had done all the stencils for 2:1. Then there were troubles with my trusty old Gestetner 466. A combination of bad stencils and bad inking produced the very faint printing which made 2:1 so difficult to read, and the old problem of not inking on the right hand margins was back with a vengeance. So that, folks, is why the repro on 2:1 was so bad. I apologized in advance for the sloppy editing of that issue, so I won't go into that again.

    I was so upset by the way 2:1 had turned out that I overcame my skinflint disposition and sent my mimeo to the shop for an oil change and a tune up. I even got fired up briefly about going from mimeo to offset, but selling my present equipment, which I would have to do in order to purchase an offset press, just wasn't possible on short notice so we're stuck with mimeo for now. But I think you'll all agree that the quality of reproduction in this issue is quite respectable for mimeography. (I'm going out on a limb with that statement, since the stencils for 2:2 have not even been cut as I write this, much less run off; but I did rough out a cover stencil and run it through the machine with impressive results, and I hope the text does as well.) The upgraded quality of reproduction in this issue was made possible not merely by having the mimeo machine worked on, but also by replacing my faithful old Selectric I with a jazzed up Selectric II. My new machine not only types with carbon ribbons, it also changes from pica (10 characters per inch) to elite (12/inch) spacing at the flip of a lever. My old machine typed only in the pica mode, and in the first four issues under the smaller format I was able to get 60 spaces per line, 56 lines per page, only by having my typed copy photographically reduced about 40%. In this issue, using elite spacing and narrowing the margins as much as possible, I have managed to get almost as many spaces per line and lines per page with no reduction whatever. Though there are about 16% fewer words per page, I think the greatly enhanced readability more than compensates for the loss. And I have partially compensated for the word loss by adding an additional four pages to the issue. I had previously established that the maximum number of pages I could mail out without exceeding the three ounce limit was 60. I can just barely squeeze another sheet in if the P.O. gives me the benefit of a doubt, but 64 pages represents the absolute limit unless some advertising revenue begins to come in to defray the increased postage and materials costs involved in going to the four ounce limit of 88 pages. I'll have to pick up about $50 in advertising revenues to pay for this increase, and to do that I've got to charge pretty high rates or else the extra pages will be all ads, and I sure as hell don't want that; the whole point of increasing the size is to increase the space available for articles and such, not to provide sellers with a virtually free method of reaching a couple of hundred mystery buffs. So, I hereby announce the inflated ad rates for TMF. Full page: $10; half page: $7; quarter page $4; eighth page and smaller: $2. At these rates I can put out an 88 page issue every time I have five full page ads. I will run the ads as they come in, one or two or however many per issue, and whenever the ad revenue reaches $50 I'll put out a large issue. Idaally, five pages of ads every two months would give us 83 pages of text, but I doubt that will happen anytime soon.

One other way to increase the issue size is to increase the subscription rate, the logical increase being 25¢ per issue. There will have to be an increase, anyway, if the P.O. goes through with its announced intention of raising rates again, so be forewarned that TMF may be $9.00 per year next year, instead of the present $7.50. I'll keep you posted.

Everybody seems to be crowding around to pat Dover and E.F. Bleiler on their collective back, and I am happy to join the throng. Together, they have contributed immeasurably to the genre and they (continued on p. 62)

THE MATT HELM SERIES

A Collaboration by
R. Jeff Banks and Guy M. Townsend

Excerpt from a letter from Guy Townsend to Jeff Banks:
I would like to use your Matt Helm chart in the next TMF, but there are a few things I need to clear with you first. Coincidentally, I did a similar "study" of the Matt Helm series of the most recent issue of my apazine, *Views, Reviews and Miscellany*; I began it with a 600-800 word essay on Helm and his career, and then went on to give tiny reviews of each of the novels in which I, like you, pointed out locations and villains. What I propose doing, if you are amenable, is combining our two works and publishing this as a collaboration; I'd like to use my essay substantially as it stands (that is, the portion of my "study" which considers the character in general rather than the specific episodes) as an introduction to your chart. . . . I have a vague impression that our views on politics may differ somewhat, and I do make a vague political reference or two in the essay, so you may not want your name associated with it, but I really don't think it's so bad as all that. Anyway, you can judge. . .

Excerpt from a letter from Jeff Banks to Guy Townsend:
Your idea of a collaborated treatment of the Helm Saga is a fine one, very appropriate as we all know "collaborators" in the political sense are just a cut away from spies. As to politics, mine seem to be about those of Hamilton/Helm, well to the left of such prominent American political thinkers as George Wallace, Mickey Spillane and John W. Campbell but far to the right of anybody likely to ever land national office again. I doubt that is going to make us any difficulty.
  Your series summary-preface is fine, so far as I'm concerned, except that Helm's sex life & views on it are (I think) considerably more realistic than you suggest. True, he does bed many women, but is almost always suspicious of their motives for bestowing favors—a hallmark of the series' realism—and I believe it the most realistic of all major U.S. spy series. Perhaps you could publish the preface as is, but interpolate my cavil on this one point. . . .

† † †

THE MATT HELM SERIES

Late in World War II Matthew Helm, a six-foot-four bean-pole of a young man, was recruited into a special secret murder group headed by a man called "Mac" which sought to hasten the war's end by eliminating select Nazis by whatever sneaky or underhanded means might come to hand. When the war ended Helm met a proper young girl named Beth while in the hospital recuperating from wounds, and married her (after resigning from Mac's outfit and being supplied with a false military record). He settled down in Santa Fe, New Mexico, acquired a few children, and supported himself and his family by writing westerns and doing occasional photography jobs. [In later books in the series he sometimes claims to have been a free-lance photographer during this period, doing writing only on rare occasions.] After fifteen years as a civilian he gets drawn back into the business through no choice of his own, and his wife discovers what he really did during the war and fastidiously decides to divorce him. This leaves Matt free to resume his career with Mac (whose real name, we learn late in the series, is Arthur Borden), and agent Matt Helm, code name "Eric", is back in the saddle, so to speak.

In the eighteen years since the series began there have been eighteen Matt Helm novels, all published by Fawcett. Twelve were published in the first nine years, and only six have appeared in the last nine years.

The novels generally follow a pattern. Matt is given incomplete instructions, often involving the assassination ("touch", in the parlance of Mac's agency) of some enemy agent who has made a bother of himself and vaguely hinting at mysterious goings on. The nature of these instructions usually means that Matt must proceed largely by intuition, which he does with a remarkable degree of success. There is always one (sometimes more) woman in the case who is not what she seems to be and with whom Matt is usually sharing a bed—or a flat bit of ground—by the time the echoes of the "How do you dos" have died down. Helm likes women who wear high heels, stockings, sexy dresses and other artifices, and dislikes pants on women. Sex is purely recreational with him and his women friends (and enemies), most of whom are in the same business as he is, though not necessarily on the same side. One of Matt's favorite and most reliable tricks is getting himself captured by whomever he is out to kill—it's often the easiest way to get into the enemy camp. He also often scans the headlines of newspapers to see if he can match up the public aspect of the case at hand with the private. His relationship with Mac is both close and distant. He is unquestionably Mac's best agent, and Mac makes use of him accordingly, but he is not just a hired hand to his boss, though Mac would never admit otherwise.

Characters often carry over from one novel to the next, though they have a habit of getting killed off after two or three appearances.

Helm is a man with a job to do and he's not squeamish about what it takes to get it done. He kills people from ambush, shoots men in the back, tortures one woman to death, shoots unarmed people, and in one instance even deliberately kills a U.S. agent to insure that the mission does not get off the track. He is the practical, efficient spy, doing his job because it is necessary for his nation's security. Not that he has any illusions about the U.S. being the epitome of Good and being incapable of error; but he does feel that it deserves protecting and that it is, on balance, a better place than Russia or China. His lack of fanaticism enables him to see his counterparts on the other side for what they are --dedicated professionals doing a job for a cause in which they believe, not depraved monsters--and to treat them with respect and, occasionally, perhaps something approaching affection.

† † †

TITLE & DATE	PLACES	VILLAIN & V's EMPLOYER	VILLAIN'S PROJECT
Death of a Citizen (1960)	WESTERN & Mid-Western U.S.	(Code Name:) Tina U.S.S.R.	Get MH to help her elude Mac's agents, leaving her free to carry out a planned killing.
The Wrecking Crew (1960)	SWEDEN--- D.C.	Caselius U.S.S.R.	Escape Mac's plan for MH to eliminate him, so that he can go on being the *best* enemy agent + as a bonus, get MH's photos of Swedish defenses.
The Removers (1961)	NEVADA--- D.C.	Martell (the Syndicate, but it's really a front for) U.S.S.R.	Force MH's ex-wife's new husband to help with drug-running operation thru threats against his family + covert smuggling of makings of A-Bomb.
The Silencers (1962)	Southwest U.S.--- Mexico	Wegmann (& his "front" Cowboy) U.S.S.R.	*Dr. No*-type sabotage of our SW tests of intermediate range missiles timed to discredit/destroy our atomic testing program.
Murderers' Row (1962)	Eastern Seaboard	Robin Orcott Rosten & Ivan Haakonsen U.S.S.R.	Maintain possession of Dr. Michaelis & AUDAP, the superweapon that would ruin submarines as offensive weapons.
The Ambushers (1963)	"Costa Verde" DC The Ranch SW U.S. & Northern MEXICO	Heinrich von Sachs, Self-Employed	*Thunderball*-type nuclear missile attack & b.mail of US w/eye toward establishment of Nazi dictatorship in the Americas.

HELM'S PARTNER	HIGHLIGHTS	REMARKS
None	MH's struggle to protect his family from knowledge of his WWII record—his confrontation with Mac in Texas—Tina's death.	Author, with half a dozen each non-series spy & western books already published, came to the series a well-developed talent.
Aurora (Sara Lundgren), Vance	MH's fight against the sword-cane of Raoul Carlsson—assassination of Wellington in MH's hotel room—reminiscences about WWII spy training.	As in *Death of a Citizen*, the author's concerns with autos & the early stirrings of Women's Lib & women's fashions play an important part.
None, tho a fellow agent is killed early-on	Performance of Sheik, 1st of several memorable dogs do appear in this series—MH's strong self-control—Confrontation between MH's ex wife & new girlfriend.	This book set the pattern of titles used later in series. Hero's attitude on gambling is realistic. MH lost original knife in this one.
Mrs. Gail Hendricks (an amateur)	Early fight in Mexican bar—MH's gimmicked boot-heels & belt buckle—the missile strike	Gail rea-pears in a small way in later books. MH lost his original pickup-camper in this one. An unchronicled job in Cuba comes between this book and next.
None	MH's early killing of a woman fellow-agent—defiance of Mac—escape at sea	More suspense & surprisingly unpleasant reversals of fortune for MH in this than in any two others. Last irregular title.
Sheila + Vadya (USSR)	Shooting of El Fuerte—MH tortured in a home workshop—machete duel.	MH is as coldly efficient as ever, but the same can't be said for many of his associates. Very rich in allusions.

TITLE & DATE	PLACES	VILLAIN & V's EMPLOYER	VILLAIN'S PROJECT
The Shadowers (1964)	New Orleans, FL & points between	Karl Krock, Self-employed Emil Taussig U.S.S.R.	Avenge death of von Sachs / sabotage U.S. defenses by assigning assassins to follow key U.S. personnel.
The Ravagers (1964)	CANADA—DC—Nova Scotia	Hans Ruyter, Naomi, Gaston Muir U.S.S.R.	Use a top scientist's estranged wife & secrets she has stolen to embarrass/weaken US.
The Devastators (1965)	Northern SCOTLAND —DC— London	Dr. McRow & Madame Ling Red China / Vadya U.S.S.R.	Use a new strain of bubonic plague against the "Free World" / delay use of this biological weapon.
The Betrayers (1966)	HAWAII—DC	Irina, Monk U.S.S.R. / Mr. Soo Red China	Hinder (in most spectacular possible way) U.S. troop movements to Vietnam.
The Menacers (1968)	Mexico—New Mexico	Vadya, Harsek U.S.S.R. / Priscilla Decker, rival	Discredit the U.S. in Latin America, with special discredit to MH & his agency.
The Interlopers (1969)	CANADIAN & US West Coast—DC	Hans Holts U.S.S.R. / Mr. Soo Red China	Assassinate the President-elect / get secret information.
The Poisoners (1971)	L.A.—Mexico—Southwestern US.	Mr. Sapio, the Mafia / Nicholas, U.S.S.R. / Mr. Soo, Red China	Try to keep MH's agency from taking an interest in Mafia activities / use sabotage to persuade U.S. to ban the internal combustion engine.

HELM'S PARTNER	HIGHLIGHTS	REMARKS
Jack Braithwaite (temporary)	MH's enlistment of an unwilling girl accomplice—amateur treatment of a bullet wound.	Begins with death of MN's girlfriend Gail.
None, tho some FBI men get in his way	Overpowering of 2 armed prison-breakers—MH surprised/interrupted in the bedroom—deaths of Naomi.	MH's encounter with Canadian thugs is reminiscent of *The Spy Who Loved Me*.
Claire + Les Crowe-Barham of Brit. Sec Svc.	Fight in MH's London hotel room—daredevil driving—end of Dr. McRow's laboratory.	This one mirrors *On Her Majesty's Secret Service*. Another assignment, on the Riviera, came between this book & the next.
Isobel Marner (amateur)	Fight in the canefield—MH getting shot with his own gun *almost* the way planned.	MH is much more spy than a counterspy in this one, with Monk's network the recognized U.S. agents in the Islands.
None	Guns & gas sparring with russians—escape in the air.	Herbert Leonard's first attempt to take over all U.S. spy agencies, including Mac's
None	The trick dog collar—MH's quick-succession fight with 3 enemies.	Hank, a very nice black Labrador retriever, is vital to MH's cover.
Charlotte Devlin (T-woman)	A hit-man's gun-firing lesson—Mr. Soo's Charlie Channish Oriental wisdom—MH's berserker vengeance.	In some ways, the most interesting book in the series: the Reds are attacking our auto industry (a favorite DH target); MH talks (often) like one of DH's western heroes.

TITLE & DATE	PLACES	VILLAIN & V's EMPLOYER	VILLAIN'S PROJECT
The Intriguers (1972-1973)	Mexico--- SW U.S.--- FL & points between	Herbert Leonard (head of rival U.S. super spy agency	Eliminate Mac, Eric & as many people as possible from the agency. Elect a U.S. Pres. by blackmailing rivals with secret info.
The Intimidators (1974)	The Bahamas, Florida	Morgan, Mr. Manderfield & Robin O. Rosten U.S.S.R.	Assassination of MH. Gaining of oil concessions in an "emerging" nation.
The Terminators (1975)	NORWAY--- Florida	These two and Helm's partner practically impossible to identify even at expense of giving away story. Masquerade/identity is subject, along with the complicated nature of truth and the settling of scores, old and new. One completely valid view is that operation (tho not book) is a put-on.	
The Retaliators (1976)	Southwestern U.S.--- MEXICO	Ernemann, a top hired assassin / Mr. Soo Red China	Frame a number of Mac's top agents as "double-agents" + kill 3 important men in Baja.
The Terrorizers (1977)	Southwestern Canada	Joan Market & Dr. Elsie Somerset, Canadian terrorists / Heinrich Glock, The Mafia	Bomb assorted public places / Kill a man & avoid agency conflict with the Mafia.

HELM'S PARTNER	HIGHLIGHTS	REMARKS
Martha Borden (Mac's daughter)	Ambush at sea—elimination of H. Leonard—philosophical arguments	As in *The Betrayers*, MH finds every man's hand against him. Very tight suspense. Mac's real name revealed.
Ramsey Pendleton UK SecSvc + Fred	MH's knife vs. 2 hired thugs—seagoing kidnapping—escape from Cuban Navy	This is the MH Bermuda Triangle book. Morgan's mid-book misbehavior is counterpoint to MH's (off-stage) in *The Poisoners*.
←	Death of Madeleine, MH's original partner & his vengeance—interrogation of Dr. Elfenbein—raid on Kotko's stronghold.	Second MH Scandinavian adventure. Captain Henry Priest reappears. Northsea offshore oil is the overt goal, making this a fuel crisis book.
Norma, from the agency + Ramon Solana-Ruiz, Mexican counterspy	Cat & mouse games on rural roads—nighttime shootout in the desert—the final shootout.	Mac's double talk briefing is clever, but bogs early story down as helm has to explain all to the reader—interagency rivalry again is prominent—Hamilton pontificates on rampant racial pride & use of political hostages—harkens back to *The Ambushers*.
Sally Wong, from the agency + Mike Ross RCMP & Kitty Davidson (sometimes)	Helm's kidnapping & turnover to the baddies by his fiancee—his imprisonment & torture in a mental hospital—escape & disruption of the place—escape from a ship.	The matter of Helm's amnesia (admittedly a hoary chestnut) is better handled than most reviewers admit—the cover identity (Paul Madden, photographer) has failed before the story begins—predictable & not among the best of the series.

PROFESSOR WITHOUT A PSEUDONYM
By Larry L. French

When is a mystery writer not a mystery writer? When he describes himself, perhaps, "simply as a writer"! It is difficult, yowever, to appripriately describe an Edgar award winner as "simply a writer", but Robert B. Parker explains: "I don't perceive myself as a mystery writer. . . . I am not much interested in mystery, but I am interested in character and human behavior, and a particular kind of attitude about maleness which too few people understand."

A professor of English at Boston's Northeastern University who is now on leave of absence to concentrate on his writing, Robert B. Parker has created "the hottest detective since Lew Archer"; his name? Spenser.

Spenser's fourth adventure, *Promised Land* (Houghton-Mifflin, 1976), which depicts the weightlifter, jogger and gormet cook retrieving a runaway wife from the clutches of the women's lib movement, and, in the meantime, preserving her husband's life from a relentless and ruthless loan shark, won the 1976 Edgar as best novel. Spenser has three earlier adventures to his credit: *Godwulf Manuscript* (1974), *God Save the Child* (1974) and *Mortal Stakes* (1975). The fifth adventure, *Judas Goat*, which takes Spenser to Europe where he is joined by Hawk (from *Land*) in an attempt to bring some terrorist types to bay, and is climaxed at the 1976 Olympic Games, will appear during the summer of 1978. Parker is currently working on Spenser #6, which "is as yet untitled" but promises to be another winner.

Professor Parker was recently featured in an article appearing in *The Chronicle of Higher Education* (March 28, 1977) entitled "The Mysteries of the Pseudonymous Professors", written by Joseph Barbato. He and other college professors were noted for their "extra-curricular" writings (detective/mystery and gothic fiction), which would not normally be included in a sabbatical assignment. Parker liked the *Chronicle* article, but he did not find it particularly interesting that a professor writes fiction; but "all publicity is good publicity". He feels that the story was well written and intelligent and the source is prestigious. Parker, of course, writes under his real name and obviously enjoys the notoriety.

Parker doesn't write short fiction. He is rather prolific, however, because in addition to his Spenser series, he has completed (with his wife, Joan) an autobiography entitled *Three Weeks in Spring* which will appear on February 14, 1977, which Parker says "is the best thing I ever did. It is, as one person felicitiously put it, a non-fiction love story." He has also completed a non-Spenser adventure story entitled *A Matter of Honor* which is currently being marketed. Parker serves on the editorial board of *Studies in American Fiction* and is a contributing editor for *Boston Magazine*. He has written two textbooks and several articles relating to his principal field, literature.

On "fiction", Parker comments: "All fiction works best if it examines people *in extremes* and mine does too, but the crime, or whatever, is merely the occasion for the action of the hero. And his action is merely the dramatization of his character. His character is what interests me."

On winning the Edgar Parker remarks: "The Edgar was the first thing I'd won since my regiment was awarded the Sygman Rhee medal in Korea. I was trying to be sophisticated and cool about it, but my throat got very dry when the time came to announce what the awards master referred to as 'the big one'. I was very pleased to win."

Parker cites Chandler and Hemingway as being most influential on his writings, but he also feels that Spenser developed as well from Rex Stout, Faulkner, Hammett and the movie classic, *Shane*. Some assumptions about the nature of the American hero were derived from reading Richard Chase, R.W.B. Lewis, Leslie Fielder and from Parker's own imagination. Twain, James and Frost were also influential, but not as much so as Chandler and Hemingway.

As a matter of fact, Parker is quoted in the *Chronicle* article as saying: "I missed Phillip Marlowe so much that I thought I'd invent my own." His doctoral dissertation concerned the novels of Dashiell Hammett, Raymond Chandler, and Ross Macdonald.

Social comment is very prevalent in *Promised Land* and some reviewers have been critical because of it. Actually, such comment is prevalent in all of Spenser's adventures, but *Land* seems to address the topics more directly, involving extensive discussion between Spenser and his female companion, Susan Silverman. In *Manuscript* element is present, in *God Save* suburbia is examined, in *Mortal Stakes* morality is scrutinized, and in *Land* "love and marriage", as well as radicalism (which is ever-present in all four books), are discussed at length.

In all four "adventures" the female element plays a

critical role, with women's liberation a constant undercurrent. Parker has noted that much of American fiction has been about men without women. Barbato quotes Parker as explaining: "I'm trying to work out some fictional patterns that one rarely finds in American fiction. . . . I want to write about love. I want to see if the American hero can be complete. If he can be a whole man without losing the values of childhood. If he can move into an adulthood that includes the power to love as well as the power to kill."

Spenser operates out of Boston and could be adequately described as sensitive, good-hearted (but tough), and unbelievably competent in what he does for a living. Spenser appears satisfied that he could probably do nothing else better, although he is really not too sure why he does it. He isn't as complicated as it would seem, however, and a point made in *Land* was that Silverman was trying to "over-complicate" him when it really wasn't necessary to do so.

Spenser (who is a real physical fitness nut) loves beer (Astel . . . hard to get), is a Red Sox fan, lives simply (except for his eating habits), and has a conscience of which his mother would be proud. He's loyal, but not beyond reason; he's tough, but not beyond sympathy; and he is certainly likeable.

Robert B. Parker has clearly established himself as a competent and talented writer of fiction. The "professor" may not consider himself a mystery writer per se, but he has certainly enhanced the genre by the development of an exciting new character, plausible story-lines and high adventure, involving people who are, to say the least, interesting. May Spenser continue a long life!

† † †

(continued from p. 18) with both new and old books of many of the speakers, and the autograph sessions provided each speaker with a pleasurable case of writer's cramsp, I'm sure.

A large art exhibit organized by Frank Eck displaying the works of many of the artists who were featured at the convention was on display on Saturday and Sunday. Many of the paintings were hauntingly familiar as they had been used for paperback covers of dust jackets. However, seeing the original paintings was a rare treat.

This year, Bouchercon IX will be held in Chicago the weekend of October 13th. Setting superstition aside, Friday the 13th will begin a mystery treat no mystery fan will want to miss!

BOUCHERCON VIII
"MURDER AT THE WALDORF"
October 7-9, 1977

By Mary Ann Grochowski

Bouchercon, for any of you who have not yet experienced this extremely pleasurable occurrence, is an annual convention for mystery and detective fiction authors, fans, aficionados, film buffs, and mystery lovers in general. Originally scheduled to honor the late Anthony Boucher in 1969, the convention has continued to flourish year after year as mystery fans welcome the chance to meet fellow mystery lovers and learn from the experience of successful authors as they discuss various aspects of the mystery novel, film, illustrations, etc.

For Bouchercon VIII, held in New York on October 7, 8, and 9th, 1977, Otto Penzler and Chris Steinbrunner did an admirable job in attempting to provide something for everyone, and by the reaction of the audiences at the various events it was evident that their hard work had been successful.

For most of the non-authors in attendance, myself included, the greatest pleasure was the honor of meeting their favorite authors, conversing with them on an informal basis, as well as obtaining their autographs. Imagine the irreplaceable experience of sharing cocktails and informal conversation with scores of famous authors and editors such as John Ball, Christianna Brand, Dorothy Salisbury Davis, John Lutz, Barry Malzberg, Edward Hoch, Francis Nevins, Phyllis Whitney, Joan Kahn, Eleanor Sullivan, Michele Slung, Jon Lellenberg, Robert Briney, Chris Steinbrunner, and Otto Penzler, to mention only a few who were present at the Friday night introductory cocktail party. Follow that with the thrill of being able to shake hands with Frederic Dannay (Ellery Queen), watch magic tricks performed by Walter Gibson (Maxwell Grant), and being kissed by Isaac Asimov! Over the three days of the vonvention many more authors than fans were in attendance. The only difficulty in getting to know anyone was having the courage to get close enough to them to read their nametag and be sure you weren't mistaken about their identity.

The informal nature of all of the speaker's presentations plus the question and answer periods with the audience afterwards made everyone feel at ease and a part of the discussion. A whole article could be written about any one of the topics discussed, but here are some of the highlights as I saw them.

Al Nussbaum, once one of the FBI's ten most wanted men, now a mild-mannered, balding, smiling-faced mystery writer, was impressive in his efforts to portray the average convict as nonviolent and somebody's father, uncle, or brother who simply was too greedy. Nussbaum got his start writing mystery stories while in prison serving his term for bank robbery. He credits prison with giving him the time and Dan Marlowe with giving him the encouragement to continue writing.

Brian Garfield, tall, slim, ruggedly handsome, and looking as if he could have been the "dude" on a western movie set, was vehement in his protestations against the movie script of *Death Wish* which he denied had much at all to do with his book of the same title. In fact, he even wrote the producers of the TV stations asking them not to show the movie on TV or at least not in prime time when children could see it because of its blatant endorsement of vigilante violence. Garfield does not believe in censorship per se, but he does believe that the public should demand less showing of violent scenes both in movies and on TV. He also asks that authors write without portraying unnecessary violence particularly when writing for public visual media. He encouraged authors to consider the moral consequences of their plots.

The presence of Frederic Dannay, substituting for Lee Wright, on the panel discussion of "What I Want—Confessions of Mystery Editors" was a saving grace. Admittedly, Michele Slung's questions as moderator of the panel were at times rather difficult and somewhat tactless, but, on the other hand, since the original panel members—John Kahn and Eleanor Sullivan—knew the topic of discussion beforehand, one would think that they could have anticipated some of the areas to be discussed and prepared answers. Eleanor Sullivan, a tall, tired looking woman with long, blonde hair, had particularly little to contribute. It would seem that as editor of *Alfred Hitchcock Magazine* she could have had much more to offer. John Kahn, editor of Harper's, was much more able to answer Michele's questions, but was reluctant to discuss any of her favorite authors for fear of offending members of the audience. She did mention her disappointment that Helen Eustis after writing the prize winning novel *The Horizontal Man* did not follow up with any other mysteries. (In fact, Eustis did publish another mystery, *The Fool*

Killer [Doubleday, 1954], but it suffered greatly in comparison to her first.) Frederic Dannay, a small, professorial looking man, balding, wearing a full beard, and large, dark-rimmed glasses which served to enhance the twinkle in his eyes, stated that a story from a current author, in order to be selected for *Ellery Queen Magazine*, should be one which reflects the times and standards of today, has originality, and would be enjoyed by the reading public. Both Dannay and Kahn spoke about the public's failure to respond to short stories in book form. Hardcover anthologies apparently do not sell, which is a shame since much of the expertise of the mystery story is in the short story form.

"The Spawn of the Shadow", which was supposed to be a panel discussion by Lin Carter, Walter Gibson, Ron Goulart, and Steranko, ended up being a nostalgic trip into the days of the pulps by Walter Gibson, introduced and commented on by Lin Carter, with assistance from Chris Steinbrunner. It is unfortunate Goulart and Steranko did not arrive to contribute, but the discussion which did take place was fascinating nonetheless. Walter Gibson, a tall, heavy-set man with gray hair and a full flushed face, looked very healthy and vibrant and is no doubt a brilliant, imaginative man with a fantastic memory.

Many more events were scheduled for Saturday afternoon and evening, including Phyllis Whitney speaking on Gothic novels, Robert Fish speaking on Cheating Customs, Hi Brown on "How I Invented Radio Mystery", and Barney Beck speaking on the creation of sound effects.

Saturday night saw the American premiere of *The Eye of Siva* by Sax Rohmer, introduced by Robert Briney and presented as a dramatic reading. Unfortunately, the stilted language of the play, the remoteness of the setting of the Far East as compared to the Waldorf, and the limitations of the "stage" in use, did not produce the suspenseful mood a Rohmer story should create. Instead, the play was amusing.

Very suspenseful indeed was the movie *Green for Danger* with Alaister Sim and introduced by Christianna Brand, who wrote the book of the same title which was the basis of the movie. Christianna Brand, an English mother earth with big baby blue eyes and short curly gray hair, was enchanting as she punctuated her commentaries with "Dahling" and the behind the scene knowledge of the making of the film.

The Saturday morning events were no less impressive for being saved till last. The first presentation was an interview with "Sherlock Holmes" staged by Julia Rosenplatt, author of the *Sherlock Holmes Cookbook*, and Baker Street Irregulars Ely Liebow, Julian Wolff, and Jon Lellenberg, with New York lawyer John Lisenmeyer posing as Sherlock Holmes. The panel's questions were very a propos and Holmes' answers witty, sharp, and worthy of the Great Master.

Isaac Asimov was the second speaker for the day. Smiling, he listened to Otto Penzler's introduction while seated in the audience with his arms around two women. When the introduction was complete, he slowly made his way up to the speaker's platform, greeting several women with hugs and kisses on the way while the audience watched bemused. Then he animatedly told the fascinating and amusing tale of how he came to be a "mystery writer". He told of several rejections of his mystery stories, with his first novel, *A Whiff of Death*, finally being published in paperback and not selling. Today this paperback is considered a rare book and is quite valuable. Still, he persevered until finally his short stories began to appear in *Ellery Queen Magazine*. One series of short stories about "The Black Widowers" is now available in both hardcover and paperback and was based on the meetings of a group Asimov belongs to. He also succeeded with *Murder at the ABA*, in which he does a tongue in cheek but surprisingly realistic caricature of himself as the character Isaac Asimov in the novel. His informal presentation was witty, amusing, and very entertaining.

The third presentation on Sunday was a panel discussion of "The State of the Mystery" by Dorothy Salisbury Davis, Edwarch Hoch, Aaron Marc Stein, and John Ball. It was a lively discussion of the development of the mystery story and the emphasis on changing times as reflected in the evolution of the mystery novel.

This was followed by Gahan Wilson's witty commentary entitled "Monsters I Have Known and Loved".

The Sunday afternoon luncheon banquet featured The Specialty of the House: a Stanley Ellin Roast during which many of the speakers from the convention took turns toasting and roasting Stanley Ellin, who appeared to enjoy every minute of it.

Besides all of the discussions, Friday and Saturday evening old films were presented until 2:00 a.m., and Friday evening was the American Premiere showing of *Silver Blaze* with Christopher Plummer as Sherlock Holmes. There were Shadow films, Charlie Chan and Bulldog Drummond films, and many more. Certainly something for everyone's taste.

The book room was well supplied (continued on p. 14)

MISCELLANEOUS MYSTERY MISH-MASH
PART II: THE CALIFORNIA SWITCH
By Marvin Lachman

For reasons best known to those who make movies, a surprisingly large number of mysteries, when filmed, have their locales switched to California. At a time when most movies were filmed in "Hollywood", this was probably due to a desire to reduce location costs. Thus, the 1950 version of Thomas Walsh's *Nightmare in Manhattan* became *Union Station* with Grand Central Station losing out to Los Angeles' railroad terminal. Twenty-five years later, Hollywood television ran another transportation switch when they filmed a TV movie version of Dorothy Uhnak's *The Bait*. In the novel, Mrs. Uhnak, herself a former NYC Transit Policewoman, has her heroine apprehend a sexual pervert on a New York subway. In the TV version, the action takes place on a Los Angeles bus.

Barnard's Crossing, a Massachusetts suburb, is the location for Harry Kemelman's Rabbi David Small series. The TV series, ecumenically called *Lanigan and the Rabbi*, is set in Southern California, at least from the palm trees and California license plates I spotted in those episodes I've seen. More surprising was that on the same night in 1976 that I watched the first of the Rabbi series, I found Sherlock Holmes also turning up in Southern California. True, it was only as a klutzy L.A. motorcycle policeman named Sherman Holmes who has a mild delusion in a TV film, *The Return of the World's Greatest Detective*. Attempting to cure him is "Doc" Watson, a psychiatric social worker. A good idea, if not original, since in the earlier film, *There May Be Giants*, Joanne Woodward plays a psychiatrist named Watson trying to cure George C. Scott of *his* Sherlockian delusion.

Los Angeles may be where most films have actually been done in this century, but San Francisco is almost universally (except fy Angelenos) admitted to be the most picturesque city in the U.S. Its hills, harbor, bridges and fog have always held a great appeal for film-makers. Even books originally set in Los Angles are shifted up the California coast. An early example was the 1935 film version of Erle Stanley Gardner's *The Case of the Curious Bride*.

The Gordon's F.B.I. novel *Operation: Terror* is set in Los Angeles and has a climactic manhunt at the Coliseum during a football game between the Rams and the Baltimore Colts. Filmed as *Experiment in Terror*, the locale is San Francisco, and the climax is at a baseball game in that city's Candlestick Park.

John Ball's Virgil Tibbs is the most famous fictional member of the Pasadena (a small city just north of Los Angeles) Police Department, but he keeps getting moved around. In both the book and the film versions of *In the Heat of the Night*, the action takes place in the deep South. However, in the film Tibbs is credited to the *Philadelphia* police. Two sequels, on film, *They Call Me Mr. Tibbs* *The Organization* transferred our hero to the San Francisco Police Department.

Carolyn Weston has written several books about Casey Kellog and Al Krug, policemen in Santa Monica, a small coastal community just west of Los Angeles. When her books became the very successful *Streets of San Francisco* TV series, even their names were changed (to Steve Keller and Frank Stone, respectively) to protect no one as far as I can tell.

Los Angeles to San Francisco is only about 450 miles. Film-makers are willing to move fictional characters much further to get them to San Francisco. Alfred Hitchcock transplanted the characters in the Boileau-Narcejac novel *The Living and the Dead* from France for his *Vertigo*. Could it have been jet lag which made Walter Matthau so weary in the Martin Beck role in *The Laughing Policeman*. This film version of the mystery by Sjöwall and Wahlöö of Sweden, about the murder of all passengers on a city bus, was shifted to the Golden Gate.

Since it is well known that New York City is losing many of its industries, it is to be expected that it will also lose some of its mysteries. Although he does not call it Manhattan, it is clear to me that Ed McBain's 87th Precinct is located there. Yet, his detectives have been scattered to the celluloid winds. His *King's Ransom* became *High and Low* and was filmed in Japan. *Ten Plus One* moved to the French Riviera as *Without Apparent Motive*. Finally, *Fuzz* retained its linty title--but in Boston.

Gordon Cotler's *The Cipher* and Max Ehrlich's *First Train to Babylon* were filmed respectively as *Arabesque* and *The Naked Edge* with London settings.

However, it is to--you guessed it--San Francisco that New York most often loses its mysteries. William McGivern's *The Darkest Hour* is about crime on the New York docks and tells of a former policeman, just released from Sing Sing. When his book was (continued on p. 24)

THE (VERY TEMPORARY) RETURN OF SKULL-FACE
A Review by Robert E. Briney

The Return of Skull-Face by Robert E. Howard and Richard A. Lupoff. West Linn, Oregon: FAX Collector's Editions, 1977. 5-96 pp.; $9.75 (regular edition), $17.00 (special edition). Illustrations by Stephen E. Leialoha. Introduction by Frank Belknap Long.

    Before we get to the book at hand, some history is necessary. Robert E. Howard (1906-1936) was a prolific writer of pulp-magazine fiction of all kinds. His unfettered imagination and natural story-teller's gift made his writing very popular during his lifetime, although he achieved book publication only once, shortly before his death. He is known today primarily as the founder of the modern sub-*genre* of "sword and sorcery" fiction. Thanks to paperback and comic book revivals of his character Conan the Cimmerian, book editions of his pulp stories and previously unpublished manuscripts are widely available in English and in many foreign languages. (At this writing, there are more than forty Howard books in print in English.)
    Howard was also an omnivorous reader, and often paid his tribute to his favorite writers--who included Talbot Mundy, Harold Lamb, Robert W. Chambers, and Sax Rohmer-- by echoing their styles and preoccupations in his own stories. His principal bow toward Rohmer was in a novella called *Skull-Face*, serialized in *Weird Tales* magazine, October to December 1929. After Howard's death the story became the centerpiece of the omnibus collection *Skull-Face and Others* (1946), published by August Derleth's Arkham House. (This book, which took fourteen years to sell out its original edition of 3000 copies, now commands $200 and up on the rare book market.) *Skull-Face* has recently been reprinted in England, but is not currently available in a U.S. edition.
    The title character of *Skull-Face* and its sequel is Howard's version of Fu Manchu: a criminal mastermind controlling a world-wide organization, dedicated to the downfall of Western civilization, served by henchmen of various ethnic categories, headquartered in opulent apartments hidden within waterfront slums, holding in thrall a beautiful Eurasian girl who falls in love with

the story's hero. . . . A more familiar collection of ingredients could hardly be assembled. The imprint of Howard's own predilections (and his intended market) can be seen in the facts that Kathulos of Egypt is given a more overtly fantastic background than Fu Manchu, and that the story is liberally strewn with headlong action scenes and hand-to-hand battles. It is pulp adventure of better than average quality.

Howard planned, and even began writing, a sequel to *Skull-Face*. However, in one of its frequent periods of belt-tightening, *Weird Tales* changed to a bimonthly schedule and stopped using serials. Feeling that this removed the most likely market for the story, Howard abandoned it, and the uncompleted manuscript rested in his files for the remaining six years of his life. It came to light many years later through the efforts of Glenn Lord, literary agent for the Howard heirs. One unsuccessful attempt was made to have the story completed by another writer. Finally, a couple of years ago, arrangements were made with science fiction writer and critic Richard A. Lupoff to have him finish the story.

Lupoff is the author of the remarkable novel *Sword of the Demon*, based on Japanese mythology, as well as of *The Triune Man*, *One Million Centuries*, and several other science fiction novels and shorter works. He has written two book-length studies of Edgar Rice Burroughs. He is familiar with, and sympathetic towards, the works of Howard and Rohmer, and with pulp fiction in general.

The result of his posthumous collaboration with Howard is *The Return of Skull-Face*. Here the story is told in the third person, rather than the first person narration of its predecessor, and the setting is an isolated sea-side castle in the north of England rather than London's Limehouse. But the story opens with the same weird atmosphere, headlong pace, violent action, and pulp prose as the original. People who dismiss all pulp writers as purveyors of "purple prose" are missing an essential fact. For the great pulp writers--of whom Howard was certainly one--the purple prose was a natural mode of expression, flowing smoothly and effortlessly in the service of the story-teller's art. Attempts by more thoughtful and careful writers to imitate the almost instinctive language of the accomplished pulp writer are rarely successful. And so it is with *The Return of Skull-Face*.

The image that sprang immediately to mind on passing from the Howard to the Lupoff portion of the story was that of sliding on an ice patch on the sidewalk, and the sudden lurch to a halt when you come to the place where the ice gives way to bare cement. (The join, by the way, occurs at the top of page 52 in the text. This is not stated in the book, and its identification comes not from any feat of subtle literary analysis but from the fact that I once had the opportunity to read Howard's original typescript of the unfinished story.) Within a few pages, characters are acting and talking in ways that just do not fit the parameters established in the first half of the story. And within a few more pages, Lupoff has committed the colossal *gaffe* of killing off the Nayland Smith surrogate in his cast of characters. His companion, the action-oriented narrator of the first story, goes into an unconvincing and embarrassing *fugue*, and the story lurches off at a tangent, contradicting facts established in *Skull-Face* and leaving loose ends of the plot flapping in the breeze. The smuggling that was going on off-shore from the castle is never explained, nor how Kathulos came to set up his elaborate subterranean headquarters in such an out-of-the-way place, nor how he has regained dominance over the lovely Zuleika who, at the end of *Skull-Face*, was happily if figuratively snuggled in the hero's arms (not missing or dead, as Lupoff mistakenly implies at the bottom of page 71). The action shifts abruptly from northern England to France, and culminates in an underwater hand-to-tentacle battel between the hero and a sea monster. The battle is excellently done; Howard himself would thoroughly have approved. It would have made a fine climax--on some other story.

This unsatisfactory *mélange* has been presented in an elaborately crafted hardcover book, with all the trappings calculated to attract the collector: illustrated endpapers and title page, interior illustrations, colorful dust-jacket, fine binding, an introduction by a "name" writer, and an essay (the best part of the book) by Lupoff on the theme "Is Collaboration a Crime?" The extra production values are unfortunately wasted on the awful comic-booky illustrations, only two of which (pages 19 and 43) even begin to capture the mood and ambience of the story. And no amount of extra trappings could justify the exhorbitant price being asked: $9.95 for a scant 65 pages of actual story.

As far as I am concerned, old Kathulos and his antagonists are still there on page 51, suspended in mid-motion in that subterranean chamber beneath Taverel Manor, waithing for the next act of the as-yet-unfinished drama to unfold.

Addendum (February 1978): The original *Skull-face*

has just been reprinted in an attractive paperback edition: *Skull-Face* by Robert E. Howard, Berkley Books #03708, 248 pp., $1.95. In common with other Berkley reprints of Howard material, the book contains a full-color fold-out poster of the cover design plus reprints of original illustrations from *Weird Tales* magazine. In addition to the title story, the book contains "The Return of Skull-Face" (under the new title "Taverel Manor") and two others of Howard's Rohmer-influenced stories, "Lord of the Dead" and "Names in the Black Book". "Lord of the Dead" has never before been published; the magazine to which it was sold in the 1930s suspended publication before the story could be used. There is an informative introduction by Richard A. Lupoff (different from the one in the hard cover edition). The exact point where Howard leaves off and Lupoff begins in "Taverel Manor" is once more left unspecified: here the break is at the end of Chapter 6 (page 214). The paperback is an attractively-produced and entertaining volume, and is recommended to all who can take these early pulp stories on their own terms.

† † †

(continued from p. 20) filmed in 1955, as *Hell on 'Frisco Bay*, Alan Ladd has hust gotten out of San Quentin. Ironically, in the early 1970's McGivern was writing scripts for a TV series about San Francisco's International Airport.

New York school teacher, Hildegarde Withers and her friend, N.Y.P.D. Inspector Piper, creations of Stuart Palmer, found themselves in San Francisco in *A Very Missing Person*, pilot for a TV series that never went further.

Lt. Clancy of the N.Y.P.D. 52nd Precinct, featured in such Robert Fish novels as *Mute Witness*, became Lt. Bullitt, S.F.P.D. (in the person of Steve McQueen) when that book was filmed as *Bullitt*. The main reason for shifting locales seems to have been to use the hills of San Francisco for one of the great movie car chases of all time. Unfortunately, this long sequence helped establish a trend which, judging from recent TV and films, has already been with us too long.

But things change, and according to Chris Steinbrunner in the March 1978 issue of EQMM, there may be a trend away from California. Hammett's *The Dain Curse*, originally set near San Francisco, is being filmed with a Long Island setting. In the second remake in the new Philip Marlowe series, Robert Mitchum plays the private detective in a version of *The Big Sleep* which has a London setting, rather than the original Los Angeles.

THE NERO WOLFE SAGA
Part VI
By Guy M. Townsend

Prisoner's Base [June 1952], published in 1952.
   THE STORY ::: A dwindling bank balance and frayed tempers involve Wolfe and Archie in a search for the killer of a young heiress who died a week before she was to come into her inheritance. Out of pique at Wolfe Archie takes in a female roomer; Wolfe promptly evicts her. When she winds up strangled to death Archie feels responsible, and when Wolfe declines to investigate the murder without a client, Archie declares that he will investigate it by himself, taking a leave of absence or even quitting if necessary. Almost immediately, however, Archie runs afoul of his nemesis, Lt. Rowcliff, and the idiot lieutenant takes on Wolfe as well, which leads Wolfe to declare that Archie is his client, thus committing himself to the investigation (for which he is not paid, of course, since, though he does not say it, Archie is his friend as well as his employee). There are plenty of suspects—five officers of a large corporation who are to divide the girl's sizeable holdings in the company if she dies before her 25th birthday, and a discarded husband, to mention only the most prominent half dozen—and the clue which reveals the identity of the murderer to Wolfe is both fair and neat, though one is left with the feeling that routine police investigation should have put the police on to the murderer long before Wolfe pins it on him. Still, it's a good tale.
   WOLFE ::: Once again, an embarrassment of riches. It is Wolfe's custom to sign the salary checks of Archie, Fritz and Theodore immediately after his Friday morning session in the plant rooms and hand them personally to his employees. Wolfe's own income, Archie tells us, "is well up in six figures" annually. Wolfe's foibles and eccentricities get a heavy workout in this one. On his aversion to work Archie remarks: "Work was looming, work that he could probably find no rational excuse for rejecting, and how he hated it!" One kind of work he avoided without exception: "He refuses to touch marital messes." He declines to shake hands when a woman extends hers, and in a similar vein he elsewhere remarks, "I will not have a hand put on me, gentlemen. I like no man's hand on me, and one such as Mr. Rowcliff's [who had tried

to propel Wolfe along], unmerited, I will not have." Rowcliff, incidentally, annoys Wolfe to the point where he roars at him: "Shut up!" This is after Rowcliff brings him downtown on a material witness warrant. During this outing, by the way, Wolfe carries his hat and stick. Wolfe's aversion to travel is not abated one whit by his successful return home unscathed: "One of his deepest convictions was that no vehicle propelled by machinery, from a scooter to an ocean liner, could reasonably be expected ever to reach its destination, and that only a dunce would bank on it." In another connection unrelated to travel Wolfe remarks, "I am capable of boldness, but not temerity." As for his habits, he rings for beer after his p.m. session, and he has three glasses before dinner. He breaks with his breakfast routing in this one, having poached eggs with Saul shortly after 6:30 one morning, rather than his customary 8:00 breakfast. It is not clear whether this early meal was in the kitchen or in Wolfe's bedroom. On Wolfe and words, he says "pfui" as well as "paroxysmal", he calls police headquarters "a paradise for puerility", and he refers to a woman as "a mere voluptuous irrelevance." On the other hand, Wolfe once again says "where I'm at." I am advised that this may not be ungrammatical, and I am not prepared to argue the point. But it certainly is not the best usage, and is therefore atypical of Wolfe. We are given a glimpse of Wolfe's political leanings at lunch when he "furnished me with pointed comments on all of the prominent candidates for the Republication nomination for President." He also makes reference to an interesting unrecorded event in the past: "Archie. You may remember that I once returned a retainer of forty thousand dollars which a client named Zimmermann had paid me, because he wanted to tell me how to handle his case instead of leaving it to me." A couple of other items: "He chuckled audibly. He doesn't do that often, and after all the years I've been with him I haven't got the chuckle tagged"; "Wolfe inclined his head a full half an inch, for him an elaborate bow"; finally, Wolfe's weight is said to be "four thousand ounces", 250 pounds, so he is really wasting away to nothing at all. Oops--forgot to say that the yellow p.j.s are present in this episode.

ARCHIE ::: Archie is very much involved personally in this case. The responsibility he feels for the girl's death is heightened by a later development, and he is so determined to play an active role in the apprehension of the murderer that he not only tells Cramer everything (with Wolfe's consent), but he actually considers offer-

ing himself to Cramer "as a special for the case. I
might have done it but for the fact that Rowcliff would
probably be giving some of the orders. Nothing on earth
could justify a man's deliberately putting himself under
orders from Rowcliff." In fact, however, Archie does
later get taken on "as an informal adjunct of the NYPD,"
and he gets "credentials signed by a deputy commissioner". Nor is Archie's help to be scorned: Wolfe says to
the D.A., "You have had . . . the services of Mr. Goodwin . . . , which is a great advantage when his head is
on straight." Elsewhere, when he does not know Archie is
listening, Wolfe states: "As you know, he is not indifferent to those attributes of young women that constitute
the chief reliance of our race in our gallant struggle
against the menace of the insects. He is especially vulnerable to young women who possess not only those more
obvious charms but also have a knack of stimulating his
love of chivalry and adventure and his preoccupation with
the picturesque and the passionate." Archie mentions his
"early boyhood in Ohio", and elsewhere aludes to a "summer vacation in Ohio in my high school days." Archie
smokes a cigarette in this one, which I believe is a
first, and he refrains from drinking while on the job,
which he has not done before: "I had myself a tall glass
of water--not that I don't like something with more authority in off hours, but that hour was far from off."
Another first in this episode is Archie's use of crude
language: worked up by his feeling of responsibility for
a woman's death, Archie says, "I will not go home and sit
on my ass while waiting for Mr. Wolfe to have a fit of
genius." He has never spoken like that before, and, it
should be noted, Wolfe is not present when he says this.
Archie makes "considerably" more than Cramer makes, and
"at least four times" as much as Purley Stebbins. Archie
says, "Ordinarily, unless there's a job on, I don't go to
the office until the morning mail comes, somewhere between 8:45 and nine o'clock." He also says, "Ever since
a certain regretable experience some years back, I never
left the house on an errand connected with a murder case
without taking a gun." He carries two different guns in
this episode (only one at a time, of course): the Marley
.32 in a shoulder holster, and "a snub-nosed Farger on my
hip." He also wears a straw hat in this one, which I believe is the first mention of head gear for him. Lastly,
there is this: "Awakened by it [the phone] at night, I
do not tell it, 'Nero Wolfe's residence, Archie Goodwin
speaking.' For one thing, I am too indignant at the interruption, and for another, I am only one-fifth awake

and not absolutely sure who or where I am. 'Yeah?' I said bitterly."

OTHER REGULARS ::: Among those just mentioned are Lily Rowan (with whom Archie spent a weekend in the country), Theodore, Fred and Orrie. Lon Cohen supplies information and Archie offers to buy him a steak at Pierre's, but he ends up having dinner at the brownstone where (after the meal, of course) Wolfe questions him extensively. Fritz, of course, is present in the brownstone throughout, as usual. Saul plays an important role in this one, though most of it is off-stage. "Saul Panzer looked less, and acted more, like the best all-round operative in New York than any other candidate I had ever seen or heard of . . . . He was always Wolfe's first choice when we had to have help." "There is nothing impressive about Saul. He is undersized, his nose and ears are too big, and his shoulders slant. With Saul a thousand wrongdoers had made the mistake of believing what they saw." "Saul cleared his throat. He's always a little husky." Nathaniel Parker [note that he has gotten his correct name back] also is a significant character in this case, and we learn a good bit about him. He is "the only lawyer Wolfe has ever sent orchids to," and Archie himself says that a person who has Parker as his lawyer "couldn't possibly do any better." Parker, "who is six feet four with nothing to protect his bones from exposure but tough-looking leathery skin", reciprocates Wolfe's respect—Archie says "he would give Wolfe his right eye if necessary." He is also a bachelor and "well and widely known for his particular taste in women." Cramer is unusually, indeed remarkably civil to Wolfe and Archie in this one, believing, for a change, that they are telling him the truth, and calling Archie by his first name. When Cramer tells Archie that the girl is dead Archie remarks: "Inspector Cramer is no Sir Lawrence Olivier, but I would not previously have called him ugly. At that moment it suddenly struck me that he was ugly. His big round face always got redder in the summer-time, and seemed to be puffier, making his eyes appear smaller but no less quick and sharp. 'Like a baboon,' I said." Of Cramer's cigars Archie says "He never lit one." If Cramer is more subdued than usual, Rowcliff certainly is not. Cramer tells Archie, "You have the same effect on him as a bee on a dog's nose." Not only does he (falsely) arrest Archie for impersonating an officer, but he also pushes his way into the brownstone past Fritz and storms up to the plant rooms and arrests Wolfe as a material witness (again falsely). Wolfe calls him "your champion ass." Archie says "There has never been a time when the sight of Lieutenant Rowcliff of Manhattan Homicide has done me good. Circumstances under which the sight of Rowcliff would do me good are not remotely imaginable." Archie also mentions that on 3 April 1949, "by order of Commissioner Skinner, you [Rowcliff] signed a written apology to Mr. Wolfe and me." Archie also mentions his tendency to stutter when excited. Purley Stebbins is also present. "I will not claim that Purley loves me, but at least he will listen sometimes." Archie also remarks, mistakenly, that "our intimacy, not social to begin with, had never reached the peak of a joint meal." In fact, they had dined together in *In the Best Families*. In the present episode they have fried clams together at Louie's. D. A. Bowen has a bit part.

PHYSICAL ASPECTS ::: Archie gives the address as 914 West 35th St. Inside, we are told that the south room is directly above Wolfe's bedroom. Fritz's room in the basement is mentioned again, and there is a door from the basement to the street in front. The location of Wolfe's chair (and desk) in the office can be guessed from the following passage: "Wolfe marched in. On account of the crowd, he had to bear right to the wall and follow it to his chair." Further evidence on the arrangement of the furniture in the office is provided by a comment by Archie about Cramer: "Instead of going for the red leather chair he was taking a yellow one, indicating that I and not Wolfe was it this time." Lastly, the front room has a rug on the floor, which is rolled up and sent to the cleaners in this episode. The big globe, I forgot to say, is also mentioned.

ROUTINE AT THE BROWNSTONE ::: Latest on the doorbell: "Ordinarily, unless instructions have been given, Fritz answers it." As a result of Rowcliff's barging in, Wolfe says "Never again an unbolted door. Never!" Meaning, of course, that the chain bolt should be on at all times. The following refers to liquid refreshments for guests: "It was a strict rule that for an evening gathering in that house, whatever the business at hand, assorted drinks must be available, and Fritz and I always collaborated on it unless I was too busy. It always got into an argument, with Fritz insisting that two wines, a red and a white, should be included, and me maintaining that wine was out because it puts Americans to sleep and we wanted them awake. We were about ready for the usual compromise--a couple of bottles of white." Archie says of Wolfe, "It was his custom, when a gathering was expected, to stay in the kitchen until everyone had assembled," at which time Archie would summon him by pushing the button on Wolfe's desk, "one long and two shorts."

ODDS & ENDS ::: "The bank balance is at its lowest point in two years" (Wolfe); it isn't improved by this case, since there is no fee. Archie tells us that, "Altogether four murderers have slept in the south room--the last one was a Mrs. Floyd Whitten, some three years ago." "Among the unwanted articles that had been introduced into that house in some sort of container were a fer-de-lance, a tear-gas bomb, and a cylinder of cyanogen." Wolfe's "eighteen-carat opener" sees some action in this one, and Archie tells us that as a bookmark Wolfe uses "a counterfeit ten-dollar bill which had been autographed in red ink by a former Secretary of the Treasury in appreciation of services rendered." The deceased in this episode is a staunch feminist. Lastly, this is, I believe, the first case in which one of the characters claims to have read Archie's accounts of earlier cases.

"Invitation to Murder" (latter half of 1952], published in *Three Men Out*, 1954.

THE STORY ::: Though he takes his time getting to it, Mr. Herman Lewent suspects that his sister was murdered a year earlier by one of the three women who worked for her invalid husband. The motive--to clear the way for marrying the bereaved widower (and the considerable estate he inherits from his wife). Lewent wants Archie to render an opinion--as to which of the three ladies is guilty. Archie goes with Lewent but before he can discover anything he finds Lewent dead in his room (he lives with his brother-in-law) from a blow on the head. This hurts Archie's professional pride, a murder being committed right under his nose, so to speak, so he confers with Wolfe and determines to try to solve the murder before calling the police. When several more hours bring him no closer to the truth Archie decides to take drastic action --he gets Wolfe on the phone then pretends to get knocked unconscious. This brings Wolfe rapidly to the scene of the crime and, though he is infuriated with Archie's subterfuge ("That was one of the two or three times, possibly four, that I have seen him speechless. He didn't even glare."), he sets to work and solves the case before the night is out. An entertaining tale, though the murderer is not particularly hard to spot.

WOLFE ::: Wolfe's laziness is again mentioned ("He hated to work"), he says "pfui", and "he disliked tilting his head to look up at people." Of his reluctance to leave the office on business Wolfe says to Archie: "You regard my rule not to leave my house on a business errand as one of the stubborn poses of a calculated eccentricity. It is no such luxury; it is merely a necessity for a tolerable existence. Without such a rule a private detective is the slave of all the exigencies of his neighbors, and in New York there are ten million of them. Are you too headstrong to understand me?"

ARCHIE ::: All we learn of him is that he has a date to spend the weekend with Lily Rowan, and that this case, which transpires on a Friday, causes a delay in his plans.

OTHER REGULARS ::: Lily and Saul are merely mentioned. Cramer and Stebbins are present at the murder scene. Archie speaks of "Inspector Cramer's round red face," and he says that Purley "has called me Archie eight times over the years in fits of absent-mindedness," which really isn't fair to the good sergeant.

PHYSICAL ASPECTS ::: The red leather chair is said to be "three steps from the end of Wolfe's desk."

ROUTINE AT THE BROWNSTONE ::: "I'm not supposed to disturb him when he is up in the plant rooms."

"This Won't Kill You" [October 1952], published in *Three Men Out*, 1954.

THE STORY ::: Pierre Mondor, Parisian chef and restauranteur who we met back in *Too Many Cooks*, is staying as Wolfe's houseguest during a visit to New York. "He got the notion, God knows how or why, that Wolfe had to take him to a baseball game, and Wolfe's conception of the obligations of a host wouldn't let him use his power of veto." Accordingly, Wolfe, Archie and Pierre journey forth to the Polo Grounds for the seventh and deciding game of the World Series between the Boston Red Sox and the New York Giants. The game turns out to be more than anyone bargained for, however, and before it is over several baseball stars have been drugged and another murdered. While the game is still going on, but before the murder is discovered, Wolfe is hired by one of the Giants' owners to find out who doped several of his players, which he does, revealing the murderer's identity as a bonus. The story has one scene, involving Archie, of an uncharacteristically pulpish flavor, but Wolfe solves this one with a neat bit of psychological observation.

WOLFE ::: Since Wolfe goes to the game as host to Mondor, this does not breach his proscription against leaving the house on business, despite the fact that he later does conduct business at the ball park. Nevertheless, such an outing was a remarkable thing, and Archie wasn't entirely pleased about it: "There were too many people, some of them alive and loose, who felt strongly that he [Wolfe] had already lived too long. He is seldom out in the open, easy to get at, and when he is I like to be nearby." There are other hazards, of a less lethal nature, to Wolfe's appearing in public: "As we went up the concrete steps [during the game] . . . a shout came from somewhere on the left. 'Go get 'em, Nero! Sick 'em.!'" As Archie does not record Wolfe's reaction we are left with the task of imagining it for ourselves. Wolfe spends the entire afternoon and evening in the clubhouse, "dining," as he sarcastically puts it, on mass-produced sandwiches and drinking beer directly from the bottle: "Paper cups had been supplied, but he hates them." He says "scoundrelism" and "pfui", and makes the following observation: "The requisitions of the income tax have added greatly to the attractions of mercenary crime."

ARCHIE ::: Archie tells Wolfe [not seriously] that he "resigns"; Wolfe responds with "Bosh". He remarks that, "with the training and experience I have had, I can report a day of dialogue practically verbatim," and elsewhere he says, "I have a routine habit of wearing a gun when I'm on a case involving people who may go to extremes."

OTHER REGULARS ::: Commissioner Skinner is mentioned, and Archie talks to Purley over the phone, but Cramer is not involved since the Polo Grounds does not lie in his part of the city. Instead, Wolfe has to contend with "Inspector Hennessy of uptown Homicide. . . . Some two years ago he had told Nero Wolfe that if he ever again tried poking into a murder in his territory he would be escorted to the Harlem River and dunked." This earlire confrontation is not a part of the recorded Saga.

ODDS & ENDS ::: "Emil Chisholm, oil millionaire and part-owner of the Giants, considered himself deeply in Wolfe's debt on account of a case we had handled for him a few years back." Once again, there is no record of this case. Archie speaks of one of the characters having "a light blue Curtis sedan." What's a Curtis?

† † †

(continued from p. 35)
He cuts himself in on their plans, but murder is not originally on the agenda. It's hard to say how stupid men can be over women, yet granting a bit of leeway, I suppose they can make messes of their lives as easily as this. (B minus)

MYSTERY*FILE

SHORT REVIEWS BY STEVE LEWIS

Claire Taschdigian, *The Peking Man Is Missing* (Harper & Row, 1977; 280pp.).

Real life mysteries that have never been solved are always the source of endless speculation. Take, for example, the fossils of the so-called Peking Man. Somebody did, at any rate, for they disappeared without explanation 36 years ago, and no one has seen them since.

This version of what really happened is completely fictional, but it can't help but be convincing, since the author is the one personally responsible for packaging up the ancient bones for the trip to safety in the United States that they never took. The background is filled with fascinating details of life in an occupied China during the first days of World War II, and what might have been turned into a story as dry as dust instead maintains the excitement generated by a top-notch detective thriller. An Edgar nomination is suspected. (A)*

Arthur Maling, ed., *When Last Seen* (Harper & Row; 337 + xi pp.; $10.95).

A welcome treat for fans of the detective short story is the annual anthology compiled on behalf of the Mystery Writers of America. Invariably each volume is built around a given theme, and this year all the stories are about missing persons of one kind or another.

The crime involved isn't always murder, but the disappearances of loved ones can leave as much impace on the lives of those left behind. The best stories are of this kind, and include those by Pauline Smith, Stanley Ellin and Ross Macdonald. The latter features an early Lew Archer, incidentally, and is redeemed from run-of-the-mill pulp fiction only by a strong ending.

Some stories are intended as puzzles only, and these have more widely varying degrees of success, with only a longish teaser from Vincent Starrett really worth mentioning. Nevertheless, as an editor Maling is to be highly commended for the wide set of variations he introduces into what could have been a fairly restrictive set of stories. A short-short by Bill Pronzini, nearly unclassifiable, merits inculsion only on a technicality, but it is a gem not to be missed. (Overall rating: B)*

* Reviews so marked have appeared earlier in the *Hartford Courant*.

Diana K. Shah, *The Mackin Cover* (Dodd Mead, 1977; 217 pp.).

  A pleasing addition to a growing list of female sleuths is magazine reporter Lindsie Hollis, who in her first crack at detective work finds herself hot on the trail of a missing pro quarterback. The effort is convincing, and the wit is genuine, but while the male-female relationship grows ever more complicated, the mystery behind what may or may not be an actual kidnapping attempt seems to fall apart through holes of its own intricate nature. The result is flawed, but the story is far above average. (B)*

Ragan Butler, *Captain Nash and the Honour of England* (St. Martin's, 1977; 159 pp.).

  The sights and sounds of 18th century London are vividly reproduced in this, the second major case of England's first private detective. His inquiries on behalf of a convicted duelist take him both high and low, as he traces back the connection between the foul squalor of the underworld and the fringes of power surrounding King George's court. And yet, although he discovers that scandal can reach even the royal bedchamber, the detection involved in uncovering the king's secret is nil, nor at this late date would there seem to be many to really care. (C minus)*

Charles Alverson, *Not Sleeping, Just Dead* (Houghton Mifflin, 1977; 207 pp.).

  Joe Goodey is a private eye. Being a cynic comes with the job, but along with a sour view of the world and a nasty way of saying his mind comes an unquenchable sense of justice that not even the soul-scouring impact of group therapy can touch.
  What he's hired to do, and what he does, is to learn who caused the death of wealthy man's granddaughter at a Big Sur drug rehabilitation commune. He also finds once again that success does not always bring satisfaction, much less gratitude. While there are some novelistic weaknesses in his approach, Goodey's last statement on the matter is an impassioned defense of the moral point of view that explains society's continued need for incorruptable investigators who are unafraid of the truth and willing to point fingers of guilt where they should. It's not been done better since the days of Dashiell Hammett, and praise greater than that cannot be given. (A)*

Colin Dexter, *The Silent World of Nicholas Quinn* (St. Martin's, 1977; 254 pp.).

For those who like their mysteries chock-full of clues, this detective puzzle of a deaf academician who stumbles across a crime in Oxfordian setting should not be missed. Chief Inspector Morse does have an advantage, however. This novel first came out in England and was published here without being rewritten for an American audience. As a result, readers who know nothing about the British educational system and public exams may be as baffled at the beginning as they are one chapter from the end, where they should be. (B minus)*

Brad Solomon, *The Gone Man* (Random House, 1977; 278 pp.).

When Charlie Quinlan's not working as a Hollywood extra, he gets his kicks as a private eye in the city of dreams, a town not primarily noted for soft, tender feelings. The restrictions of the private eye novel being what they are, it's no surprise to find yourself reading yet another case involving the missing son of a wealthy father who finds that he's hired more help than he'd bargained for, but with non-stop dialogue as pungent and striking as this, it goes down quickly and smoothly one more time. (B plus)*

Clifton Adams, *Death's Sweet Song* (Gold Medal 483, 1955; 144 pp.)

Adams is perhaps better known as an award-winning writer of westerns, but this is one of two or three crime/suspense novels he's written as well. It's solidly in the small subgenre of the field once very popular—the story of a good man gone bad, tempted too far by weaknesses of the flesh and the over-powering proximity of the sensuous evil of an all-too-willing woman. If this is a tale no longer seen very often, Gold Medal is probably at fault, for they surely wore out their presses on this sort of eroticism during their first ten years in business, but please note that practitioners of the form do included such noted authors as Charles Williams and John D. MacDonald.

This one takes place in and around a shabby motel on Route 66, at a time before the interstate system made us a nation of Holiday Inners. Creston, Oklahoma—a town a smart guy aches to get out of, and Joe Hooper is pining away for the once-in-a-lifetime opportunity to come knocking. Beth is the local girl everyone assumes he will marry some day, taken for granted, a pinpoint of accuracy showing how life goes on in a small town. The wife of the safe-cracker staying overnight in his motel, in the room next door, is named Paula. (continued on p. 32)

VERDICTS

(More Reviews)

P. D. James, *Death of an Expert Witness* (Scribner's, 1977; $8.95).

In *Death of an Expert Witness*, one of the characters points out that love, not hate, is the most dangerous emotion. The interlaced loves of the personnel of Hoggatt Forensic Science Laboratory in East Anglia form the motivations and complications of P. D. James' excellent seventh novel, which again features Adam Dalgliesh, the cool, introspective poet-policeman who has gained a loyal following among mystery fans. Dalgliesh is called to investigate the death of Edwin Lorrimer, the senior biologist at the Hoggatt lab, which specializes in work for the police. All the scientists have strong reason to dislike Lorrimer, a fussy, prickly, but to some degree powerful, personality. Thus, each member of the staff is not only a suspect but also a person capable of misleading the investigator, and some of them do so. The complexity of the problem is augmented by the fact that Dalgliesh is faced with a "locked-house" (if not locked-room) crime, and English tradition is preserved, in a sense, in that the lab building was once an old country house, suitably isolated.

Though Edwin Lorrimer is a disagreeable character, the author makes him apprehendable and understandable because of his professional capability; his decent interest in the lab's youngest employee, Brenda Pridmore; his genuine suffering over the loss of love; and his dutifulness as a son. This ability is one of James' chief strengths as a novelist, and she exercises it in each of the many portraits in this gallery. All are sound; several are brilliant. Among the smaller portrayals are some of the strongest: Brenda, just out of school and weighing a career in forensic analysis against marriage; her mother, suddenly real to Brenda as a separate person; Alfred Goddard, who creates the local color almost on his own; and Mrs. Dora Meakin, briefly a witness and a lonely widow, desperate for companionship. These characters as well as the major figures come vigorously alive, and the reader cares about them, even when he doesn't like or approve of them.

James has won a reputation as a feminist because of her perceptive comments about the roles and status of women. That pattern continues in this novel, and the portraits of women are perhaps the most vivid here. It is to James' credit, however, that she *never* slants her comments about female characters to make a point. Like the men, they are good and bad, simple and complex, happy and sad, troubled and serene. In short, they are realistic, and it is through this realism of characterization that the novel's tension arises.

Other realistic elements provide unity and strengthen the tone of the novel. Readers meet the lab team as they begin work on another murder which forms the frame for the central story. Dalgleish repeatedly constructs a plan of action only to have it altered by the sudden availability of a witness or a scrap of new information. The scientists often think of their professional responsibility, and their sense of loneliness in the witness box serves as a symbol for the human condition.

But the overriding motif here, as in all the James books, is the idea that murder, while not contagious, is contaminating. It changes the survivors as it eliminates the victims. As Dalgliesh assures Brenda, it needn't spoil life for the sane, the healthy, but it alters the future, and Dalgliesh, like James and her readers, is ever mindful of the fact that he is an instrument of that change—healing and hurting simultaneously. *Death of an Expert Witness* is a good book. Both established James fans and new readers will like it . . . and Scrabble players may well learn a new word. "Clunch", it turns out, comes in handy for that game. (Jane S. Bakerman)

G. F. Newman, *You Nice Bastard* (New English Library, 1972).
The book opens as London's number one underworld leader, Jack Manso, is being taken by the police for questioning. Manso has been led to believe that it's all part of a deal with the authorities, many of whom are in his pay, but once in the cells he begins to have doubts. His mind then runs back to his first time behind bars, during his army service, and nearly all of the book is taken up with a description of Manso's meteoric criminal career between the two incarcerations. The final chapter reveals whether Manso's doubts were justified. The book is full of violence, verbal and physical, and is not for the squeamish. However the lasting impression, and a frightening one, is of authenticity--the same sort of authenticity that comes through in such books as George Higgins' *The Friends of Eddie Coyle*. Those who follow crime in the English press will note a remarkable similarity to a big gang trial that took place in London quite recently and the blurb reveals that the author "moved

with impunity through London's criminal circles", I can well believe it. The book took a tighter hold on me as I progressed through it and I shall take all possible steps to obtain the earlier *Sir, You Bastard* about police corruption and some of the same characters. (Bob Adey)

Pat McGerr, *The Seven Deadly Sisters* (Doubleday, 1947; Collins, 1948).

Miss McGerr's highly acclaimed first novel *Pick Your Victim* (1946) was innovative in that it immediately revealed its murderer, but left it to a stranded group of marines (and the reader) to hear the evidence and determine the victim.

The author's second novel, *The Seven Deadly Sisters*, attempts to repeat and improve upon what she knew to be a successful approach, and the results are extremely rewarding. I think that *Sisters* almost attains the same level of excellence as its predecessor.

Sally Bowen, a recent arrival to England with her journalist husband, Peter, receives a letter from an old school friend expressing sympathy for the notoriety engendered by the murder of her uncle by her aunt.

Unfortunately, there are no further illuminating details, and Sally has exactly seven married aunts.

She is unable to sleep that night fearing the possible unstability of a few of her relatives might be inherited by her unborn child. Her aunts are quite a collection of characters, and they have more than their share of problems.

Sally tells Peter all she knows about her aunts from the time she came to live with them until she left for England some half a dozen years later.

Comes the dawn, the narrative ends, and Peter knows who killed whom. His solution is soon confirmed by a short drive to London, and a visit to a library's newspaper file.

In some ways *Sisters* is an advance over *Victim*. The characterizations are deeper. The pace is swifter. The framing device is more deeply embedded into the fabric of the narrative. There's also a high degree of skill present that is able to involve this reader into the constant arguments of a feminine household.

I must confess to a spectacular lack of ability in attempting to solve detective puzzles, but in this case it was childishly simple. (Charles Shibuk)

J. C. Masterman, *An Oxford Tragedy* (Gollancz, 1933).

An Oxford Tragedy has been praised by Barzun & Taylor

and other devotees of the academic mystery as a masterpiece. It is certainly successful in presenting the milieu of an Oxford college, where an unpopular tutor is murdered in the Dean's rooms. Ernst Brendel, a visiting Austrian lawyer of European reputation who has occasionally helped the Viennese police, acts as amateru detective more plausibly than in most Golden Age books--that is, he subtly tries to determine the facts without either impeding the official police or taking over himself. Francis Winn, sixtyish Vice President and Senior Tutor of the College, narrates the tale, frequently chiding himself for his ineffectuality. The characters are (for the most part) well delineated, the pace is leisurely, the atmosphere is convincing. On the whole, a very satisfactory book. (Jeff Meyerson)

A. S. Burack, ed., *Writing Suspense and Mystery Fiction* (The Writer, 1977).

If you have any dreams of someday becoming a writer, you should read this book. If you enjoy reading what writers have to say about their craft, you should read this book.

The articles range from very broad topics to the nuts-and-bolts practicalities of writing.

I especially likes Stanley Ellin's "Irony and Surprise", Joe Gores' "Short Fiction--With a Difference", Edward D. Hoch's "Plotting the Mystery Short Story", Bill Pronzini's "The Elements of Suspense", Colin Wilcox's "Writing and Selling the Police Procedural Novel", and Patricia Moyes' "Mysteries Within Mysteries".

There are other fine articles by A. A. Fair, Naomi A. Hintze, Joan Kahn, Ngaio Marsh, Harold Q. Masur, Dorothy L. Sayers, S. S. Van Dine, and Raymond Chandler.

The only other book that is more helpful for the beginning writer of suspense and mystery is Dean R. Koontz's excellent *Writing Genre Fiction* (Writer's Digest, 1972).

After reading these two books, all you would-be writers need is a typewriter and tons of paper. And some luck. (George Kelley)

Robert Middlemiss, *The Parrot Man* (Fawcett, 1977; $1.75).

A well-plotted tale of intrigue which finds U.S. and Israeli agents' interests in the activities of old and new Nazis in the U.S. and Brazil on both converging and conflicting paths. The explosion which maims but fails to kill Simon de Bonneville sends him on a search for vengeance through the *invasões* of Bahia to a surprising climax in a São Paolo hotel. I found Simon's choice of a

Blue Hyacinth as the weapon to counter-balance his crippling injuries a refreshing change from the now-familiar arsenals of spies and counter-spies.

Many first novels are like the German Volkstrum Carbine of World War II, "brilliantly designed but poorly executed". *Parrot Man* is not. The plot is carefully designed and smoothly executed, and far more plausible than that of *The Boys from Brazil* (to which the cover blurb compares it). Detail and local color are effectively used to enhance the narrative rather than as props to support it. Perhaps most importantly, at least to me, the characters are believable; I cared about what was happening to them.

For those who have enjoyed Bagley, Deighton, Le Carré and MacLean, I recommend *Parrot Man*. Read it, you'll like it. (David Doerrer)

Geoffrey Household, *Rogue Male* (1939), *Watcher in the Shadows* (1960), *Red Anger* (1975) [all reprinted by Penguin in 1977 at $1.95 each].

For nearly forty years now Geoffrey Household has been writing the same novel over and over again--and getting away with it. In this novel the hero's life is in danger from some sinister source from which he is unable or unwilling to go to the police for protection. His response is either to go to ground (quite literally, in *Rogue Male*) or to serve as his own stalking horse to capture the enemy singlehandedly. The hero shows a great reluctance to resort to violence, and it is one of the weaknesses of the stories that the hero is often able to predict with confidence what his unknown opponent will do. E.g. (I'm making this up, but it's true to form), "I knew that I could move around freely for eight to ten days since he would not care to try another attack before then."

When I was a child, dragged to church against my impotent will, I used to pass the interminable hours (so it seemed, at least) of the preacher's sermons by drawing fanciful pictures and diagrams on the backs of church programs. My favorites were of underground installations —aircraft landing fields built into the faces of cliffs, underground cities, self-sufficient subterranean dwellings, etc.--and nothing reminds me more of those youthful escape attempts than the novels of Geoffrey Household. He is a master story teller, so if you want a good entertaining yarn, and your ability to suspend disbelief is functioning properly, you may want to take advantage of Penguin's commendable reissue of the Household tales. (GMT)

THE DOCUMENTS IN THE CASE
(Letters)

From Jeff Banks, Box 3007 SFA Sta., Nacogdoches, TX 75962: Thanks for your latest issue. Enjoyed most of it, as I always do. But at the risk of making it look as though I dislike Geo. Kelley (which I don't) I'm going to disagree with him again. The key to a point, perhaps over-subtle, that Garfield wanted to make in *Death Wish* is aptly stated in Kelley's review. He says (on p. 6), "I'd rather be tried in the United States for any crim (sic, but it's probably your typo [*mea culpa*]) I'm accused of than in any other country in the world." Sould would any criminal! We've become so permissive that the law, courts, etc., no longer serve as a deterrent to crime. Thus, vigilantism is an answer that must suggest itself to anyone capable of self-defense. Behind that point, and later in the sequel especially, Garfield rejects that response just as thee & me & Kelley, but that does not mean that the problem (lax laws, courts & enforcement) does not exist. ¶ Let me apologize to you and to Mizz Glantz, if as I suspect, I contributed to her decision not to renew. She does quote from one of my letters, and I know that I've said unkind things about the Great Movement in such places as my *Fernanda* review. I suspect you realize much of that was intended as an attempt to stir up some controversy—certainly not to drive anyone away! ¶ Finally, let me say, perhaps paraphrasing an old racist remark, that I really have nothing against Libbies. Some of my best friends are of that persuasion, but I wouldn't want my sister to marry one. [*A later letter*] I thought I'd kept a copy of *Oui* with Garfield's reaction to the movie *Death Wish*, which also takes some trouble to explain the point of the book. And I wanted to quote a few words of that at Kelley. But I couldn't find it. Then, since mailing my letter to *MFr* I had second thoughts that the piece might be in *Gallery* where I found it easily. I'm sending you a marked copy . . . . [*What follows are the marked portions.*] "In a nutshell," says Garfield, an extraordinarily genial man in his mid-thirties, "the essential difference, to me, between the book and the movie is that the book suggests that this kind of thing could happen and that it's a dangerous possibility. The movie suggests not only that it could happen, but that it *ought* to happen. Because of this, lately I've had the problem of fending off hate mail from strangers who believe I

have created a recommendation for fascism. They probably haven't read the book. The book is *not* the film."
¶ "I would say that it was miscasting, but that's putting it mildly. In order to make that story really work, the character must be sensitive. Bronson does not project sensitivity. The worst effect his casting had on the film was to make the transition from ordinary citizen to killer almost invisible, and the transition really *is* the story. That's all the story has—the exploration of the change that takes place in this man."

From Myrtis Broset, 204 S. Spalding St., Spring Valley, IL 61362: I enclose my check for $2.50 to cover this year's subscription to "The Mystery Fancier". I am not going to let my enjoyment in your magazine be spoiled by any remarks about women. ¶ I, too, would like a report on the '77 Bouchercon—I wish I had been there, unfortunately since I was expecting guests over the holidays, I took my vacation then. ¶ The cover on January's issue was the best yet, reminiscent of the covers on the old mystery books. Art work isn't easy for most of us; for me it's impossible. ¶ Jeff Meyerson did a great job on the index, though I can't understand anyone volunteering to type lists. ¶ Dorothy Juri would like to know how your women subscribers became interested in mysteries; I can't say about others, for myself it happened because in my teens I read everything that came along, my sister bought mysteries and soon I was a devoted fan. Reading an average of two dozen books a week, I couldn't find enough new books so was forced to look for old ones. For this reason I was (and still do) constantly perusing the ads. By the way, I have never seen a soap opera whether working or not, and am an avid reader of private eye stories. I am now a legal secretary—alas, the attorneys have destroyed my illusions, none of them acting like Perry Mason, Anthony Maitland, or other lawyers in books. I like to read reviews—it is probably a good idea to stick with a reviewer who likes the same books you do—or you can read several reviews and if they all agree a book is good, buy it, or if bad, forget it.
¶ I hope your other subscribers return to the fold; they are missing out on a good thing.

From Jane Bakerman, RR 23 Box 131, Terre Haute, IN 47802: Sorry! I'm red-faced. Here is the information on the Uhnak book: Uhnak, Dorothy. *The Investigation* (New York: Simon and Schuster, 1977). 283 pp. [. . .] ¶ Now, then, Guy, I don't think that you should worry about people "rather" publishing in TAD than in TMF. The field needs both journals; we enjoy both, and should either change or disappear, I, for one, would be much the poorer! ¶ Though I haven't yet read every page of TMF 2:1, I have, as usual, forst read "Mysteriously Speaking" and "Documents" . . . and I've been thinking about Ilse Goldsmith's comments. Like her, I'm often struck by the wide range of information writers in *all* the journals seem to have; I keep reading people's intriguing comments about authors totally strange to me, and it is a little overwhelming. But I think that shouldn't stop *anyone* who is really "into" mystery/detective fiction from setting down her/his comments and sending them in. A perceptive reader is a perceptive reader, and what she/he has to say about an author or a work is going to be of interest and probably of fun and value to other good readers. While I read "old" names with great anticipation (I'm looking forward, for instance, to reading Marv Lachman's "Miscellaneous Mystery Mish-Mash" this evening), it's also exciting to find "new" names and to discover what they have to say. It seems to me that a free exchange of ideas from all directions and from all sorts of perceptions is what fanzines are all about. It's a heady combination and certainly one that most of us don't find in either pop or professional magazines.

From Michael Doran, 4117 W. 90th Place, Hometown, IL: I received my first issue of TMF on my subscription, which was Vol. 2 No. 1. Among my first impressions was "You should have subscribed much earlier." Said impression was confirmed when I got to the letters column, which made reference to a number of past articles, reviews, and letters, most notably the business of women as mystery fans. The trouble is, without seeing the original, I have no real way of determining what the original argument was in the first place. So what I'd like to know is, is there any way to get Volume One? I'll pay whatever you ask, but the point is, if possible, to send the back numbers as soon as you can, because I really want to know what I've missed. [*I trust the back issues have arrived by now.*] ¶ Before I go any further, an abject apology for not typing this, but the family machine was borrowed some time ago. We expect it back in time for the next Presidential election. I'll see what I can do about getting it back sooner. Accordingly, I will refrain from commenting about the readability of the issue I received. Although I do think you might get better results from an offset press. (If you are using an offset, give a thought to replacing the blanket. I notice that the dim spots all seem to be on the same part of the pages.) ¶ I don't care to single out which articles or reviews I liked best, because frankly they all impressed me greatly. My tastes in mysteries is fairly widespread and eclectic (two words I much prefer to voracious and indiscriminate). I learned long ago to go by the author rather than the genre, and I have no trouble going from Christie to Ross Macdonald to Ed McBain to Emma Lathen, and that's just a sample of my collection (or hodgepodge, if you will: I've also got Stout, Westlake, Queen, Gardner, dozens of others, plus a hundred or so back issues of EQMM, plus anything that catches my eye or intrigues me. I've been fighting the battle of shelf space since adolescence). ¶ I do have one question to direct to E. F. Bleiler: Who handles the distribution of Dover paperbacks in the Chicago area? The titles he mentions as having been published in October 1977 and earlier haven't turned up anywhere in Chicago that I can find. I mean, Chicago isn't the sticks, and I'd hate to think that the people at Dover think that. ¶ I hope you can help on those back issues, but even if you can't, be assured that this is one subscriber who won't have to be asked twice to renew. Best of luck in the future.

From Frank Hamilton, Box 1225, Gloucester, MA 01930: After more than a year of being well buried in the shambles I call my collection, my preview issue of The MYSTERY FANcier has miraculously surfaced into the light of day. ¶ Because of this I am now writing to you (much too late, I'm certain) in order to ascertain whether or not TMF is still being published, as I am interested in subscribing to it. [. . .] ¶ I have occasionally had my art-work appear in Steve Lewis' MYSTERY*FILE, XENOPHILE, Bob Briney's ROHMER REVIEW, WHISPERS, RBCC, Capt. George's PENNY DREADFUL among others. Many of Weinberg's early PULP CLASSICS carried my covers and illoes. I mention this as part of the explanation of my delay in subscribing. When I received my complimentary copy of TMF, I skipped through it and became highly enthusiastic over the possibility of a new outlet, with quality, for my drawings. I'm a complusive contributor, you see. ¶ My elation was short-lived, however. The editor's message, "Mysteriously Speaking", expressed very clearly that artwork was of no importance to a fanzine, and this one in particular. Unfortunately, this attitude immediately categorized me in that group that was "so put off by these remarks that [they] wouldn't even send . . . an obscene gesture." So I didn't send one . . . but I did throw the 'zine to one side where it was promptly forgotten until now. ¶ Time has mellowed me to the point where I can now accept a fanzine without art-work; particularly when it's as well-done as the first issue of TMF. I do hope you are still publishing. [*I wrote back in part--"Ouch. I am appalled that my careless remarks in the Preview Issue put you off so much. Especially since the one thing that I need most--besides substantial articles--is cover art. Consider yourself enlisted as a cover artist." As everyone has seen, Franklyn responded with a splendid portrait of William Powell as Philo Vance. A million thanks, Franklyn, and keep them coming. You and Al Fick are giving TMF a real classy look.*]

From Bob Briney, 4 Forest Ave., Salem, MA 1970:
It's good to see TMF again, even though it meant an hour or so of squinching up my eyes suitably. . . . (Many years ago, when I worked for IBM, I was told that the core planes which made up the computer's memory--many thousands of tiny iron rings threaded on fine wires--were produced in a factory where all the employees had small eyes. I think of that description every time a new TMF shows up.) At any rate, I hasten to enclose my meagre check for a subscription to volume 2. ¶ Thanks to Larry French, I now have to go searching for Roy Winsor paperbacks. Somehow, the books had not come to my attention before now, but they sound like something I would enjoy. ¶ Marv Lachman's collection of mystery oddities was enjoyable. There are other book dedications of the same ilk as the one he quotes by Brandon Bird. Christianna Brand once used a dedication womewhat on the order of "To Mary Lewis, whose work I admire"--Mary Lewis being Miss Brand's real name. And the two "George Sanders" mysteries, *Stranger at Home* and *Crime on My Hands*, were dedicated "to Leigh Brackett, whom I have never met" and "to Craig Rice, without whom this book would not be possible". Brackett and Rice were, of course, the ghost-writers of the two books in question. ¶ The mention of Edgar J. Goodspeed in Howard Waterhouse's letter rolls back the years. I remember reading Goodspeed's *The Curse in the Colophon* at the age of thirteen or thereabouts. Everything has faded from memory now but the title, and I'd love to find a copy of the book and re-read it. ¶ It's good to see some publicity for Dover's series of mystery reprints. The company has done many fine volumes. (And if they had done nothing but resurrect Collin's *Armadale*, I would be forever grate-

ful.) The one disappointment was the recent edition of Sax Rohmer's *The Dream Detective*. Someone failed to do the proper homework on that one, since the reprint was taken from a British rather than an American edition. All British editions are incomplete, containing only nine stories, whereas the U.S. editions have ten. The additional story, "The Chord in G", is one of the best of the set, too. The U.S. editions aren't that hard to come by, and in fact there was a mass-market paperback edition in the mid-60s, so the Dover reprint could easily have followed the complete text. ¶ Just received several issues of *film and filming* from England--delayed by the dock strike--and note therein some news of forthcoming mystery films. The remake of *The Big Sleep* has been completed. I don't know how I will react to the film as a whole, but already I have trouble visualizing Candy Clark in the Martha Vickers role from the original--renamed, for some reason, Camilla instead of Carmen Sternwood. (Perhaps on the philosophy that anyone who would swallow the conversion of 1940s L.A. into 1970s London would not balk at renaming a character or two.) Also on the way is another "big" Christie adaptation: *Death on the Nile*, with script by Anthony Shaffer and Peter Ustinov as Poirot. The cast also includes Bette Davis, Mia Farrow, Maggie Smith, David Niven, Angela Lansbury. The entry that boggles the mind is the announcement of a remake of *The Hound of the Baskervilles*, directed by Paul Morrissey (Andy Warhol's director and cameraman), with script by Peter Cook and Dudley Moore. Cast includes Cook and Moore (as Holmes and Watson?), Denholm Elliott, Joan Greenwood, Irene Handl, Terry-Thomas, and Kenneth Williams. Is the world ready for this?

From Jeff Meyerson, 50 1st Place, Brooklyn, NY 11231:
I didn't realize how much I missed TMF until I got the latest issue and stayed up till 2 A.M. reading it. It was quite a good issue. ¶ I can see from a couple of the comments addressed to me that I did not make myself clear last time. I did not mean to suggest that people don't buy books and series that they will not get around to reading for many years; I do it and so do a lot of people. (Incidentally, I wish Howard Waterhouse had not called attention to the Pyramid Green Door series until I found the 16 books I need to complete the run.) I meant that I didn't know of any people *without an interest in mysteries* who bought the books, either just as something to collect or as an investment (as in the comics field, for example), without ever intending to read them. To

Gerie Frazier; of course many of us find an author or series we like and run out to buy all their books, but this is different. ¶ There was a very interesting group of letters this time. Thanks to Jeff Banks for liking my reviews; I'd like to return the compliment. Also agree on Steve's reviews—excellent. I must admit that I found Dorothy Glantz's letter rather bizarre. She is as entitled to her opinion as anyone else; that goes without saying. I don't think any point of view, except the obscene or libelous, should be censored, and I know you feel the same. I can't understand what she was saying. ¶ To answer Howard's question, I collect several of the smaller series, including Pyramid Green Door, Avon Classic Crime Collection, Dell Great Mystery Library, and the Mystery League hardcovers. Completism is in the soul. For someone who hates locs, Jeff Banks' are always full of interesting things. His spy fiction course sounds good. ¶ Mr. Bleiler's letter reminds me what a wonderful job he and Dover are doing with their reprint series; I mean, 2 van Guliks, *The Department of Dead Ends*, *Clues of the Caribees* and *The Curious Mr. Tarrant*. What a treasure trove! ¶ Lastly, thanks for including PEN in The Line-Up even before the first issue has come out. I only hope it will be nearly as good as TMF. [*I wasted a lot of time trying to reply to the departed Dorothy's letter before I finally admitted that I didn't know what the hell she was talking about either and gave it up as a bad job.*]

From Larry French, 14326 Milbriar Cir., Chesterfield, MO: After a long and tiring holiday, January was a welcome sight, although the cold weather (and snow) continues. The new year was appropriately "rung-in" with the arrival of TMF 2/1, a *Baker Street Journal*, a *Baker Street Miscellanea* and Bob Briney's *Rohmer Review*. Intermixed therein, however, was the arrival of my *John Dickson Carr Memorial Journal* "Notes for the Curious" from the printer, a limited edition of 500 copies, each costing $5. Send your orders to me at [the above address]. ¶ The "Journal" features commentaries by such notables as Bob Briney, Otto Penzler, Ellery Queen, Chris Steinbrunner, Robert Lewis Taylor (author of the 1951 JDC Profile in *The New Yorker*), Al Hubin, Mike Nevins, Michael Harrison, Jon Lellenberg, Roy Winsor, Roger Herzel, Jon L. Breen, Marv Lachman, Charlie Shibuk and Joan Kahn. Biographies of both Dr. Fell and "H.M." are included, as is a listing of the "Canon of Carr". ¶ I appreciated Bob Briney's remarks as to my article on JDC. I provided Bob a copy of the pulp story "The Man Who Was Dead" (which was provided to me by Rick Sneary), by John *Dixon* Carr, and Bob agrees that it is definitely Carr and "reads like a preliminary sketch for 'New Murders for Old" (also entitled 'The One Real Horror') which appeared in EQMM, August, 1966." ¶ Ilse Goldsmith might contact Michael Gilbert directly at his law office in London (5 New Square, Lincoln's Inn, London, WC2A, 3RP England) for a checklist. Mr. Gilbert is a delightful and most helpful person. I recently obtained permission from him to reprint his article "Sherlock Holmes and the Wombles" in a future issue of BSM with an "introduction" to Mr. Gilbert written by this writer. ¶ The comments of William J. Rall, Frank D. McSherry and Jeff Banks were appreciated. E.F. Bleiler's article was most interesting as was Marv Lachman's. Under the editorship of Mr. Bleiler, Dover issued a collection of short stories by Robert W. Chamers in 1970 entitled *The King in Yellow and Other Horror Stories*. Chambers, who died in 1933, was the author of some 72 volumes and was the creator of "Mr. Keene, Tracer of Lost Persons", the book being published by Appleton in 1906. ¶ Roy Winsor informs me that he is "getting closer" to a publisher for his Ira Cobb mystery, *A Sweet Way to Die*. Our St. Louis "Noble Bachelors" convened in honor of "The Master" on the 14th and Dr. Bart Sims gave a report on the annual BSI dinner in New York. There were some excellent presentations and the latest news was that Mike Murphy's new book, *Hemingsteen* is now available for $7.95 from Mike at 7144 Murdock, Suite 101, St. Louis, MO 63119. Phil Shreffler gave it an excellent review in the St. Louis *Post-Dispatch*. ¶ Compliments to Jeff Meyerson for the "review index" and this writer is looking forward to Jeff's *Poison Pen* #1.

From Dave Gorman, 7359 Orinoco, Indianapolis, IN 46227: The MYSTERY FANc*ier* is an excellent fanzine, it really is. And I hope you can make it survive. Let us know what kind of response the ads from EQMM and AHMM bring. Whether you can break even with TMF is something else again. Buck and Juanita Coulson publish a stf fanzine called *Yandro* that breaks even and maybe even makes them a little money, but you have to subscribe to it to receive it (no free issues for letters of comment as in most science fiction fanzines), and the Coulsons have *personalities*. Which is a big factor in the success of fanzines, me thinks. Dick Geis is the reason for the success of *SF Review*. But then there is *Algol* which has hardly any editorial personality, but has Dick Lupoff's book reviews to give the reader the feeling that this fanzine/magazine is more than a fanzine/magazine, it's more like a *friend*. ¶ Unfortunately, TMF is not that strong on personality. It's not because Guy Townsend isn't capable of writing that way, as witness DAPA-EM. But I think the problem is that you are limiting the fanzine to strictly a "mystery fan" zine. I know you are limited in space, but I think it would only help (and entertain) if you would break out of the editor role and turn "Mysteriously Speaking . . ." into a conversation with the readers. ¶ The academics may not appreciate it, but I'm sure the majority of *fans* would. (even those people who don't realize they are fans.) How about an account of your trip to England next time? What do *you* think of the current mystery fanzines being published? ("The Line-Up" is hardly worth the bother. Just what the hell is *The Thorndyke File*? And is it worth, in *your opinion*, $2.50 each issue?) ¶ Write about, excuse me, *talk* about politics, books, fans, whatever you want to. It is your fanzine. Only in fandom can the editor have unrestricted rights to publish whatever *he* wants. Consider using that right, please Guy? ¶ Onward to volume 2, number 1 of TMF. It's good to see Larry French recommending Roy Winsor. Not that I have ever read him, but we need recommendations about authors and/or certain characters. With a lot of hardcovers not making it to paperback, and too many paperbacks not making it to the newsstands, I can always use a recommendation about books and authors. (On the other hand, Larry French's letter reads like a J. G. Ballard "new wave" novel. All bones, some meat, no fat at all. And I enjoy the fat, as witness the above comments.) ¶ George Kelley is my favorite contributor to TMF. He writes about authors that I care about, Koontz, Pronzini, and now Brian Garfield. *Death Wish* was a good book, a study in a typical liberal who gets pushed too far. And Garfield makes damn sure that we understand that he considers the character off the deep end. ¶ *Death Sentence* is a much poorer book. It is as if Garfield was so appalled at the audience reaction to Charles Bronson's portrayal of Paul Benjamin as a "good guy" that he wrote the second book to make sure that no one misunderstood his feelings about Benjamin. ¶ In fact, *Death Sentence* is nothing more than an apology for writing *Death Wish*, and Garfield telling us over and over again that Benjamin is not a hero, not even sane. He should have just ignored the movie and its response and not bothered at all. ¶ But *Hopscotch* and *Recoil* more than make up for DS. Writing two "nonviolent" novels in such violent settings is certainly a coup. I like *Hopscotch* better because it is a superb suspense novel that you don't realize is nonviolent till you're finished. *Recoil* is about the dilemma of a nonviolent man trying to combat with a man and organization that has no restrictions on violence. So you notice the nonkillings. ¶ Okay, Kelley, how about Parker, Roger L. Simon, and the various Westlakes? ¶ Steve Lewis' reviews may just be *The MYSTERY FANcier*'s Dick Lupoff. I think short reviews are the hardest to write well, but they can be the most enjoyable when done like Steve's. There are some books I would just as soon ignore, and others I wish he would expand his opinions on (especially the collections). I also like his rating system. ¶ The real meat and fat of TMF is the letter column. It's the most important feature of a fanzine (along with editorial you-know-what), and I'm glad to see that you are not restricting it. Lots of information, opinions, questions & answers. I wish it was longer, but for all I know you may be printing almost all the letters you receive. ¶ Listen Guy, TMF is one good fanzine. Better than TAD in my opinion. It could get better. But most of all, I hope it survives. [*You are right: I am "limiting the fanzine to strictly a 'mystery fan' zine." The thing that all TMF readers have in common is that we are all mystery fans. We are not, alas, all Guy Townsend fans. I do obtrude myself into this magazine from time to time, and for these minor indiscretions I make no apology--where's the fun of being the editor if you can't abuse the power sometimes?-- but I think it would be a mistake to convert TMF into a personalzine. I do my soul-baring and opinionizing in my DAPA-EM zine, sometimes to my considerable embarrassment. Besides, Dave, there are other readers who hold views diametrically opposed to yours; witness the following letter.*]

From Steven Stilwell, 3425 Nicollet Ave., Minneapolis, MN: Keep TMF coming, it isn't TAD, at least not yet, but I see a great future ahead for it. ¶ Do letters count as contributions? Also, have you thought of a free Book Exchange like TAD's? There's used to be much more interesting but I think people are intimidated by the format. I can't believe there are less wants & offers out there. Oh, well, TMF gets better every issue. Please don't get SF fannish, if you know what I mean. [*Yes, letters--except for one or two liners, and those which solely solicit information or other assistance--do count as contributions. I would like to do a free Book Exchange in TMF, but until*

TMF brings in enough advertising revenue to enable me to increase its size beyond the present limit of 60 pages there just isn't enough room.]

From David Doerrer, 4626 Baywood Cir., Pensacola, FL: A comment on Myrtis Broset's definitions of "mystery fans" and a "mystery collector": there is, I believe, a third type of collector (at least this is my personal approach): one who reads many mysteries (often via a library in my case) but only adds those which he/she has enjoyed well enough to read more than once. I have found this approach keeps the collection growing at an arithmetical, rather than a geometrical, rate. Unless, of course, one's favorite authors happen to be prolific, as some of mine are! ¶ The above brings a question to mind. What does Nero Wolfe do with the books he doesn't add to his library? ¶ A final comment, which I hope you won't find intrusive. Your reasons for a change of address are certainly none of my business, but I can't help but lament the move from Pidgeon Perch Lane. That had character! It was almost as good as Rayo Grande Avenue. *[Some of us are afflicted with a well-nigh insuperable reluctance to read books we do not own. When I read a book it becomes a part of me, an experience in my life, be it good or bad, and the idea of parting with it is unthinkable. (In fact, the only books I can remember ever having gotten rid of were a couple of Mickey Spillane's Tiger Mann novels; I put them where they belonged--in the garbage.) For that reason though I have a library card I rarely use it, except for books which are too expensive for me to purchase for myself. As for what Nero Wolfe does "with the books he doesn't add to his library", I would like to think that he, too, keeps all the books he reads. However, given his unspeakably barbaric habit of dog-earing his own books (though not those of others), I'm not so sure. He did mutilate and burn* **Webster's Third International,** *you know . . . . As for the change of address, I know this reveals my basic insecurity, but I was enormously relieved to move away from Pidgeon [sic] Perch Lane. While living there I was constantly fearful that people would think I didn't know how to spell pigeon. Not people in Memphis, you understand--they think pigeon is actually spelled with a "d".]*

From George Kelley, 505 N. Carroll St., #503, Madison, WI: Let's face it. ¶ It's hard when a once brilliant writer brings out a book that sucks. ¶ It's hard to review it and to say tough, true statements about a bad book by a noted writer. I've been reading Donald Hamilton and Matt Helm since the early Sixties. And it hurts to write the 1977 version of Matt Helm off as a pompous asshole. ¶ I remember Matt Helm of *Death of a Citizen*, the best Helm novel Hamilton will ever write. Donald Hamilton built a dazzling character in that book, a character who was a little gray but still tough as they make them. No long speeches, no pages of filler drek; *Death of a Citizen* had Helm as a master of controlled violence. The violence was sharp, it was real. You could feel it. ¶ But the last handful of Matt Helm books had me shaking my head with disbelief and boredom. Much as I would like to agree with Jeff Banks and Jon Breen, I believe a reviewer should judge individual books on their own merits. *The Terrorizers* is a bad book and the readers of *The Mystery Fancier* have the right to be protected from wasting their hardearned money on an inferior product. ¶ Too often a series is judged by its best books. The first half-dozen books in the Matt Helm series are very good, with *Death of a Citizen* rated excellent. But the last half-dozen books in the series are at best fair, with *The Terrorizers* rated crappy. ¶ I take no pride in reporting this. I feel sad because Donald Hamilton isn't turning out good books arymore and we are all poorer for it. ¶ Turning to another writer and review that's generated comment, I still stand by my article on Dean R. Koontz. My dissatisfaction with Koontz is that he is a better writer than some of his books demonstrate. I feel that some of his books are sloppy. Koontz could be an excellent writer. Under his Brian Coffey pseudonym he wrote a brilliant caper novel, *Surrounded*. However, none of his work has matched that standard since. Under his own name, Koontz has just published *The Vision*, a very good suspense novel. I urge you to read it. In a few months I'm planning to do a "Dean R. Koontz Revisited" article where I'll review his latest work. Yes, it's entertaining, but . . . . ¶ Lastly, I want to thank Jeff Meyerson for the marvelous job he did indexing Volume One of *The Mystery Fancier*. Indexing is dull, thankless, but endlessly convenient. Again, Jeff, thanks for a job well done. ¶ Guy, I like the mix of articles, reviews, and letters in *The Mystery Fancier*. My only suggestion is that *The Mystery Fancier* might want to conduct a yearly poll, something like the poll *Locus* conducts for the best science fiction novel. That involves the readership, is fairly inexpensive, and generates lots of controversy which makes for a lively journal. What do you think about it? [*Sounds good to me. How about it, folks?*]

From Marv Lachman, 3410 B Paul Ave., Bronx, NY 10468:
I have mixed feelings about volume 2 number 1 of TMF, with the good outweighing the bad. The letters, as always, are a high spot—the closest thing possible to conversing with other mystery fans. I continue to like your Wolfe saga, and I thought Larry French's articel on Roy Winsor was terrific; the only problem: it was too short. Incidentally, I just received a 32 page *John Dickson Carr Memorial Journal* from Dr. French, and it is well worth owning. Professionally printed, it includes articles, tributes, and a chronology of the life and works of Carr. It is apparently available (though it is a limited, numbered edition of 500 copies) from Dr. Larry L. French, 14326 Milbriar Circle, Chesterfield, MO 63017. ¶ I liked most of the reviews in TMF—especially those by Lewis, Banks, French, and Kabatchnik. Other reviews, e.g. those by Myrtis Broset of two Marsh books, could have benefited from the editorial pencil since they merely tell the plot again—except for one short paragraph of criticism. ¶ Finally, after reading more typos than I can count, I must agree with you, Guy. It was "a sloppy issue." ¶ I'm sure future issues will look better. I, for one, am mighty glad that TMF (even with typos) has made it into its second year. [*One way or another, the reproduction on this issue should be of much higher quality than 2:1; it could hardly be worse.*]

From Peter Pross, 1303 Willis St. Richmond, VA 23224:
The cover of Vol. 2 No. 1 was great—I hope Al Fick's pen doesn't dry up. Especially enjoyed reading Larry French's article about Professor Ira Cobb. Articles which incorporate or "spin off" from personal interviews are excellent vehicles for reviewing authors' books and characters, and French's article is a fine example of this vehicle. Personally, I would like to read articles of this sort and articles about famous characters, stereotypes and/or writing techniques rather than book reviews. I do enjoy reading the reviews in TMF but I think the magazine is top heavy with reviews. However, I do have respect for Steve Lewis—anyone who can find time to read and review that many books has got to be working hard. ¶ Another item which I would like to see appear in TMF is a section devoted to describing local sources of 2nd hand mystery fiction—for instance, where an out-of-state visitor can find and buy 2nd hand mystery fiction in New York City. As a dealer/collector, I am always checking out bookstores, antique shops, flea

markets etc. for mysteries. I have my own circuit of shops in the Virginia-North Carolina-Wash. D.C. area which I periodically check. No doubt, other readers of TMF do the same. I would be willing to supply information about my area to TMF's readers and I hope other readers would also reciprocate. Those who wish to keep their "little secret shop" a secret will probably not contribute, but the hell with them. Someone will find out about their secret and buy all the books anyway. So, I will make an offer to Guy and the readers of TMF--if you desire, I will write a brief section for TMF which features a particular region's bookshops etc. But, it will be necessary for the readers of TMF to send information about their area to either Guy or myself. If individuals wish to write their own article about, let's say, the book shops of Chicago, that's fine too. The point is that I would like to see TMF serve as a forum for this type of information. Next issue I will discuss the bookshops of Virginia and, hopefully, if the readers of TMF provide the information, future issues will describe other regions. [*The article[s] on shops sounds fine, especially if TMF can get enough ads to go beyond the present 60 page limit. Otherwise, such articles would have to wait for a few free pages to show up. Anyone wishing to do an article on their own area, send it directly to me; anyone wishing merely to contribute information, send it to Peter at the address above.*]

From Walter Albert, 7139 Meade St., Pittsburgh, PA 15208: I'm enclosing a tardy check for renewal of *The MYSTERY FANcier*. (You seem to be still insisting on the *FAN*. I thought you had decided to drop this after repeated violations by careless readers. I like the linguistic double-play and hope you will retain it. I also like the artwork on the cover. You do like to underline points, don't you?) [. . .] ¶ I liked the bevy of short pieces at the front of the magazine. I always enjoy Bleiler's scholarly pieces of detection and it was good to have what appeared to be an interview with Roy Winsor which promised the timely demise of the Prof. Cobb series for lack of a publisher. Winsor won the most undeserved "Edgar" in recent memory and unless the succeeding books in the series--which I didn't have the courage to read-- were better, he may have contributed to the decision by the new owners of Fawcett not to publish any more mysteries. I am beginning to discover in myself a long-overdue resistance to marginally interesting mystery fiction--and the Winsor novel was not anywhere near the

margin--brought on, I suspect, by the proliferation of
large paperbacks with movie stills and book illustrations
that endlessly rehash the same material and the mass of
fanzine book reviews that make me painfully aware that I
can never make a real dent in the hundreds of genre novels published over the years. I shall either have to
drastically limit my book purchases and library borrow-
ings or remain a quivering pulpy self-indulgent unregen-
erate slob. My puritan conscience is beginning to assert
itself once again and I dream of a select library of in-
dispensable essential texts, knowing that there's a
steel-jawed trap buried in that poetic reverie. Selec-
tion requires choice and choice is buried in quantity.
The number of reviews published in Vol. I of TMF is mind-
boggling and when you add to it the reviews in TAD, DAPA-
EM, *Mystery Monitor* and *Mystery Nook*, mad Mrs. Rochester
hears a scratching at the door indicating that she may
soon have company. In 1978, I plan to restrict myself to
work on my TAD bibliography, material I have promised to
Enigmatika, the maintenance of my newsletter for DAPA-EM
at a minimal level, and current fanzine subscriptions.
And the books I start and can't put down. You must realize that, unless I am peremptorily fired, this is "lei-
sure time" activity that must fight for time with family,
movies, other book-reading & collecting, eating and
sleeping.

From Charles Shibuk, 2084 Bronx Park East, Bronx, NY:
Reader James A. Jobst may be interested to learn that
Arthur W. Upfield's *Bony and the Black Virgin* (1959) received its first & only American publication in 1965 in
a Collier paperback edition. ¶ With all due respect to
Mr. French and his fine article on Roy Winsor, allow me
to cast a dissenting vote. ¶ I recently read *Three Motives for Murder*, and for the life of me, I could find no
merit whatsoever. I also regret to say that I disliked
it intensely. ¶ On the other hand, I enjoyed Donald
Hamilton's *The Terrorizers*, but it is of course far from
his best work. [*A later card*] Re your sample issue: I
assume that you now know that "Rober Denbie", author of
Death on the Limited, is the pseudonym of Alan Green &
Julian Paul Brodie. ¶ Green is the author of *What a
Body* (1949) which received an Edgar the following year,
& he is frequently mentioned by John McAleer in his Rex
Stout biography. Keep up the very good work on TMF.

From Jo Ann Vicarel, 2571 Eaton Rd., University Hts., OH:
Here is a check for TMF subscription. Have no time to

write but do want you to know that I for one disagree with you about the merits of publication in TAD as opposed to that in *The MYSTERY FANcier*. TAD is too much of an ego trip now; too many Ph.D.s, too many scholarly "works", too much name dropping, etc. . . . That is what happens when academia gets its meaty hands on a publication. ¶ On the other hand, *The MYSTERY FANcier* is fun to read, it is alive with interesting thoughts, informative and entertaining reading. When I went to the hospital to give birth to my daughter at the end of September, my husband noted that I was clutching the latest issue of TMF to read between contractions and La Maze breathing. What more can be said from any reader!!?? ¶ Good luck to you and may all those slow pokes who have yet to subscribe reach for their checkbooks now. [*TMF must have an affinity for medical institutions. Sandy Sandulo sent a newspaper photo of herself giving blood while reading TMF. Here's the letter that accompanied the clipping:*]

From Sandy Sandulo, W. 1518 7th Ave., #6, Spokane, WA: I thought you might like to see the extent of the value of *The MYSTERY FANcier*. As I was doing my bit for an unknown accident victim, I accompanied my quiet bleeding with a review of Vol. 2, No. 1 of the MF--don't you think that appropriate? Notice how cool and unconcerned and absorbed I appear. ¶ Not so with the young photographer who did the pic accompanying the article--shortly after he recorded me for posterity he quietly fainted, and only when I heard the soft thump did I manage to tear myself away from your publication. You do good work! [*And note the first paragraph of the following letter:*]

From David Doerrer [*Yes, I know I should have combined this with his other letter a few pages earlier, but I didn't, and I'm damned if I'll retype all these pages to cover up an editorial oversight.*]
First things first. Many thanks for the back issues of TMF. [. . .] They did a great deal to brighten a miserable week in which I was fighting a cold, flu, virus, bug or what have you. [. . .] ¶ TMF is my first exposure to a fanzine and I'm enjoying every bit of it. I've been a mystery reader, in what I realize has been a rather desultory fashion, for over 20 years and had thought that I had covered a fair amount of ground. I am now beginning to think that I've barely scratched the surface. Your desire to maintain a mix of articles, reviews and letters in TMF pleases me very much. I can manage a

letter and will even risk a review, I hope, now and then, but it will be some time before I attempt an article. I've gone through all the issues once and am working my way through again, finding something of real interest to me in every issue. (Go ahead and print that. Someone once said, "If a man does not blow his own horn, who will?") The follwoing are my observations on various items which struck me. ¶ I have to disagree with Jeff Banks on the value of letters of comment, at least to me. Art Scott's explanation of EQMM's different covers on otherwise identical issues (1:2) answered a question which had been puzzling me. Bob Briney's amplification of the Crossen checklist is certainly valuable. Bob may be right when he says that one doesn't have to be an expert on Crossen's writing to recognize the deficiencies, but one has to know a lot more than this amateur to spot them. (1:3) ¶ On page 41 of the Preview Issue you mentioned "several pages of books for sale" at the end of that issue. What happened to them? (The pages, not the books.) ¶ Concerning the various comments on the "high cost" of TMF. I spend $6.50 a month for the daily paper and throw that away the next day. I also think the first-class mailing to be rather special for any publication these days. I'm still waiting (6 weeks to date) for my first issue of TAD. ¶ I know our devoted public servants of the USPS were responsible, but as a librarian I wish you hadn't had to change format and size midway through a volume! ¶ I'm enjoying the Saga tremendously and truly appreciate your decision to reprint the first part in TMF. Keep it coming. Those who don't appreciate Nero Wolfe and company are indeed to be pitied. ¶ Hank Davis' article on Mr. & Mrs. North and the Lockridge's was also most enjoyable. I tried a "Pam and Jerry" years ago and couldn't stay with it; now I'll try again. I did enjoy several non-series character books which they did and am going to look them up for a second time. Of the characters which Richard Lockridge has continued since 1963, Merton Heimrich and company are my current favorites. ¶ Amnon Kabatchnik has me puzzled by his reference to Adam Hall/Elleston Trevor's Quiller as a "double-agent". (2:1 p. 35) I've read, I think, all of the Quiller novels to date and I can't see how this term applies. Vesper Lynn (*Casino Royale*) and Johnny Vulkan (*Funeral in Berlin*) are double-agents, but Quiller? ¶ I'm finding Myrtis Broset's reviews a bit uneven. In reviewing *The Billion Dollar Brain* (2:1 pp. 38-39), the statement that Deighton's protagonist and Harvey Newbegin are working together to "keep the Russians from obtaining the formula for keeping viruses alive in eggs" makes me wonder if we read the same book. The method of keeping a virus alive in an egg is a technique, not a formula (see p. 165 of the 1955 Putnam's edition), and the Russians want not the technique but the particular virus involved. [. . .] ¶ A couple of closing odds and ends. My artistic ability is nil. I can manage a straight line (most of the time) with a ruler and a passable flow chart with a template, but that's about it, so I can't help you with cover or interior art. I am, however, willing to type lists. Do you think it would be feasible for me to do these on stencils and mail same to you? Oops! Scratch that. I just re-read your description of the current reproduction production process and suspect that it requires equipment I don't have access to. I do have access to an IBM Selectric II and can probably get a matching type-face element. If I can do anything to help with lists, let me know. ¶ I would also be happy to do the index to the reviews in Vol. 2, unless Jeff Meyerson is planning to continue. Have you thought about an index to articles? I assume you felt there weren't enough to warrant this at the end of Vol. 1, but I think (and hope) there would be after another volume or so. ¶ The enclosed computer print-out is the full bibliographic record for TMF as entered in the data base [bank?] of the Ohio College Library Center. If you haven't seen it before, I thought it might be interesting. ¶ In closing, can you or any of TMF's readers give me an author and/or title reference for a mystery with a rather bumbling, nosy busy-body as its main character named the Honorable Constance . . . ?, who is also referred to as "the Hon Con"? I couldn't find her in *The Encyclopedia of Mystery & Detection, The Detectionary, Catalogue of Crime* or Allen Hubin's list of series characters in *The Mystery Story*. (Incidentally, I'd list those four titles plus Lenore Gribbin's *Who's Who Dunit* as my most essential reference works right now, mainly because I own the first four and have easy access to a copy of the fifth! I'm not sure they fit into your category of "essential analytical works".) [*At the time that I mailed out the first batch of copies of the Preview Issue I also had on hand a long list of books for sale, which I appended to the Preview Issue in order to save postage. Since last year's book lists are not much more valuable than last year's newspapers, I did not include the book list in copies of the Preview Issue which were mailed out later. Mystery solved.* ¶ *The method of repro employed for TMF is in a state of flux as I write these words, though it* will be resolved before 2:2 is printed, but I may well take you up on your offer to type lists. I hate the damned things--typing them, that is--and your access to a Selectric II marks you down as a prime victim, er, assistant for future list-typing assignments. I do not know if Jeff's masochistic tendencies were satisfied by doing the review index for volume one, but if they were, or if his new fanzine leaves him no time for indexing, you may take off the hair shirt and quit sleeping on a bed of nails--the index for volume two will pass to you by default. An index to articles may well be in order by the end of volume two. ¶ Query--what's a Pensacola, Floridian doing in the Ohio College Library Center? And what the hell do all those numbers and abbreviations on the print-out mean? ¶ I've given myself a headache trying to remember why the Honorable Constance should be so familiar to me, but entirely without success. No doubt hordes of knowledgeable TMFers will (smuggly) supply us with the answer in TMF 2:3. ¶ Alas, your mention of "essential analytical works" sent sharp pangs of guilt through my frail body. That was one of my little schemes which fell by the wayside (along with the idea of binding volume one into a book). A dozen or more people responded to my appeal for suggestions as to the ten most essential analytical works in our genre, but I never got around to trying to bring order out of the resulting chaos. Perhaps if someone else would like to restate the proposition--and handle all the dirty work of compiling and commenting on the results . . . ? I personally don't have the time (translation: I've got the time, but there are other things I'd much rather do with it).]*

From Myrtis Broset [*speaking of editorial oversights...*] The March, 1978 issue of *The Saturday Evening Post* contains an article titled "A Sleuth for All Seasons", taken from H.R.F. Keating's book, *Agatha Christie, First Lady of Crime*. If you have not read the book, and are a Christie fan, read this excerpt and you may tempted to buy the book. Mr. Keating remarks on many of Poirot's exploits, and goes on to describe the life of the detective. ¶ The *Post* is also running the Christie book *Death in the Air* in serial foarm. A good place to start for anyone who has not yet read a Christie book, though I don't know how anyone could miss them as the stores are full of reprints. [*I have the Keating book and think highly of it. Can anyone explain why the SEP would choose to serialize an ancient story like* Death in the Air? *I enjoyed it, mind you; I'm just mystified as to why they settled upon it.*]

From Helmuth Masser, H. Austgasse 3/25, A-8054 Graz, Austria/Österr.: I like your magazine because it somehow breathes the efforts of one man team that can rely on goodnatured help from willing friends. Yours is a very personal approach to a field we are all interested in. ¶ Unfortunately I won't be much of a contributor--despite your friendly invitations in TMF--I simply know too little to tell your readers about. Just in case you've got 2 or 3 readers/collectors of analytical material who read German I could put together an annotated list of books published in Germany dealing with crime fiction and/or crime writers. ¶ What do I like best in TMF? Well, above all the reviews and verdicts--and whenever they are controversial (on one and the same book) it's a nice thing to decide who to believe, who to side with, before trying to obtain the book. As to the articles which I would like to read in the pages of TMF I think you should go on mentioning what's being published in the States, telling us about the latest Parker or Executioner (with the occasional last Christie or Carr for those who favour them--most of your readers I guess). My favorite authors are the ones who wrote in the '30s or early '40s (often in *Black Mask* under Shaw) who have often been labeled as TOUGH GUY writers, hardboiled authors, etc. The kind of language they wrote, the colloquial, racy, slangy style, the witty (and sometimes funny) use of syntax, grammar and words that helped to create or further develop a peculiar language so different from refined, cultivated and elegant British English is THE thing I cherish. ¶ It's a pity books by these authors are so hard to come by. I envy you your second hand bookshops where you can pick up a Dell mapback with the map on its back--what treasures . . . . ¶ I have recently got a paperback copy (worn, torn, pencilled) of Richard Sale's Lazarus #7, a shabby copy but precious to me because the text is intact. ¶ And it's not a far step from these writers to mainstream literature of the Fitzgeralds and Wests and Steinbecks et al. ¶ But I see I'm being garrulous--it's just that my enthusiasm for that peculiar American idiom has carried me away. A final question and I'll be silent for another year: I have often wondered about the term "the COGNOSCENTI" (cf TMF II/1, p. 52); quite obviously it's "the people in the know". What strikes me as funny is the ending--*i*. The word's Latin--so shouldn't it rather be the COGNOSCENTES, those who know (strictly speaking it ought to be: those who are getting to know). Anyway what would be the singular of cognoscenti? A cognoscentus? A strange form, indeed--and by the way, offensive to your female readers, who might protest against the masculine endings -us and -i, seeing that they are again being represented by males, not being called cognoscentae! Just think of the irate lady from Sweden who so strongly resented you fellows-speaking-their-minds business. ¶ So please get me an explanation of this mysteriously wrong ending -i. Yours sincerely, Helmuth Masser (one of your subscribentES and not subscribentI). [*Regarding your offer to compile an annotated list of analytical works in German for any TMF readers who may also read German, I throw it open to the readership. Myself, I have always had a tremendous respect for the Austrian and German people for their amazing ability to speak and understand the German language. I subscribe wholeheartedly to Mark Twain's views on the subject.* ¶ *I am not one of the* cognoscenti, *or even the* cognoscentes, *regarding Latin, but I've always thought that "i" was a proper ending for plurals in Latin. And a quick glance at* Webster's Third International Dictionary *(forgive me, Mr. Wolfe) shows* cognoscente *as the singular and* cognoscenti *as the plural.*]

SALE list and WANT list. Prices moderate. James H. Tinsman, Gunbarrel Meadows, Apt. #204, 5117 Williams Fork Trail, Boulder, CO 80301 (continued from p. 2) deserve all the support and praise they can get. A list of their publications in our field can be had by writing to Dover Publications, 180 Varick St., New York, NY 10014. Mr. Bleiler very graciously arranged for TMF to receive review copies of the Dover mystery titles, and over the last eight to ten months I have sent them hither and thither, in lots of one to four books, to various TMFers for reviews. To date there has been a total response of one—count 'em—one review. I hope this mention will nudge the delinquent reviewers on to sending in those reviews.

Another publisher deserving a pat on the back is Penguin. Long a leading--perhaps *the* leading--publisher of mysteries in paperback, Penguin is consolidating its position by issuing title after splendid title of mysteries both old and fairly new. Penguin is reprinting a run of Geoffrey Household novels (three of which are reviewed briefly herein), and has recently produced a paperback edition of Frank MacShane's *Life of Raymond Chandler* ($3.50 and worth every penny). Another of their recent reprints is Jack London's *Assassination Bureau, Ltd.* (completed by Robert L. Fish, $1.95). I found it completely unreadable and will send my review copy to the first person who sends me a notarized promise, signed in blood, that he will review it for TMF. Also, they have put out Freeman Wills Crofts' *Inspector French's Greatest Case* ($2.50), which I hope to have read in time to review it in TMF 2:3.

As new subscribers to TMF trickle in--I would describe the response to the EQMM and AHMM ad as modest, hardly justifying the thirty-odd dollars the ad cost--the supply of back issues diminishes steadily. Volume one, number one is now out of print (and my efforts to print some more copies from the old stencils ended in ignominious failure), and I have only seventeen otherwise complete sets of volume one (including the Preview Issue). These six issues (PI + vol. 1:2-6) are available for $7.50 the set, and when they are gone that's it, folks (unless I have a hell of a lot better luck re-using old stencils). Completists who must have TMF 1:1 can try Bakka Book Store, 286 Queen St. W., Toronto, Ontario M5V 2A1, Canada. They have advertised a few copies of TMF 1:1 for $1.75 (plus 25¢ handling, plus 50¢ charge for American checks--$2.50 in all).

I have previously had occasion to comment on the disgraceful condition in which some manuscripts arrive at TMF. I presume that every one out there owns or has access to a dictionary, so there is no excuse for rampant misspellings and misused words ("antidote" for "anecdote", for God's sake!). Sure, we all make mistakes (elsewhere in this issue I spelled "smugly" with two g's, and there are no doubt many other typos which I have missed, despite my efforts to do better), but even a moderate amount of attention would make some contributions look more like they were produced by responsible adults, rather than by not over-bright third graders with literary asperations. Okay, so I'm overstating the case--Jeff Meyerson tells me I have a tendency to do this--but, damn it all, I have better things to do with my limited time than to rewrite your submissions, so take a little time to read them over before sending them in, and consult the dictionary from time to time. Most of TMF's contributors do make an effort to clean up their copy, or else they do it right the first time and don't have to clean it up, but there are a few who don't, and it is to them that I direct these remarks. And to forestall certain comments let me state that I have no sympathy for the inverted snobbery which holds such matters as correct spelling, grammar and sentence structure in contempt. If one is going to use a language, one should use it correctly. If you prefer to communicate with grunts and groans it's your privilege, but it is equally my privilege not to have to listen to you or to have to respond in kind.

While I'm in a complaining mood I may as well say a few words about reviews. About the body of the review I do not speak--there are as many different ways of writing reviews as there are people who write them, and there is no single right way to do it. But there are certain forms which need to be observed when designation the item being reviewed. I prefer the following order and format: Author, *Title* (Publisher, date of publication; price [only if a new book]). Some reviewers like to include the number of pages and that's okay (though in most cases it's also superfluous), and some even insist on including the place of publication, which, however bibliographically correct it may be, is pedantic in a magazine such as this. (After all, you or your book dealer are going to have to look up the *complete* address anyway, if you plan to order from the publisher, so what good does it do you to know part of the address beforehand? Besides, most American publishers have New York addresses anyway.) I keep getting reviews without publishers or publication dates and, while I run them, it embarrasses me to do so, and I'd appreciate it if you'd glance at the title page and its obverse when doing your reviews.

On to happier matters. John McAleer's long awaited *Rex Stout: A Biography* (Little, Brown, 1977) is now in print, and I unequivocally declare that it was well worth the wait. My own credentials as a Rex Stout fan are fairly well established, but I came away from John's book with a heightened appreciation of that most remarkable creator of Nero Wolfe and Archie Goodwin. Anyone who has ever rejoiced at the Nero Wolfe stories owes it to himself (I join Messrs. Stout and Wolfe in regretting the absence of a third pronoun in our language, but I'll be damned if I'll engage in a lot of verbal gymnastics just to avoid offending the occasional feminist fanatic, ever alert to ferret out offence where none is intended; in certain contexts, such as the present one, himself, mankind, man, etc., refer not to a single sex but to humankind as a whole—if Dorothy Ganz had not alreaded departed our ranks in a huff last issue she would no doubt do so now; tough—I'll tolerate and even try to respect differences of opinion, but I'll not pander to idiocies . . . or idiots), to read this splendid biography of a splendid human being. The price of the book is $15.00, but John has offered to pass along his author's discount to TMF's readers and will send a *signed* copy to those of you who send $12.00 to him at 121 Follen Rd., Lexington, MA 02173. That's postpaid, folks, and one of the best bargains you are liable to come across in a good long while.

I apologize for monopolizing so much of this issue with these editorial ramblings. You will see when you get to the letters section that I have been urged to spend more time editorializing, but I really did not intend to take up this much room with my comments and would not have done so had there not been so much that needed saying.

Let me finally close these remarks with a few words about the next issue. I have on hand already the second part of Peter Pross's "Raymond Chandler on Film" article. It arrived late and was too long to include in this issue, but you will se it in 2:3. Marv Lachman has promised his article on John Dickson Carr for the May issue also, and George Kelley's article on "The Caper Novels of Tony Kenrick" will be there too. That issue may be even better than this one, which would be a nice habit to get into— each issue being better than the last.

Go well, my friends.

www.ingramcontent.com/pod-product-compliance
Lightning Source LLC
Chambersburg PA
CBHW031426040426
42444CB00006B/702